Servant
to the Slave

Servant
to the Slave

Mary Slessor

Catherine Mackenzie

CF4·K

Christian Focus Publications Ltd. Geanies House, Fearn,
Ross-shire, IV20 1TW, Scotland, Great Britain.
www.christianfocus.com
Cover design by Owen Daily and Daniel van Straaten
Illustrated by Andrew Lloyd Jones
Printed and bound by Norhaven AS, Denmark

*Author's note: Some vocabulary in this book is native Scots. This reflects
the vocabulary Mary would have used. Dialogue has a strong influence
in this text and must be read as fictional. It is used to retell facts of Mary
Slessor's life and show facets of her character. This is a story of the life of
an amazing woman. She has hinted at various events in her childhood,
through letters and diary entries. I have tried to fill in some of the gaps
in a way that aids the reader to a further understanding of Mary Slessor,
the child, the woman, the Servant of God and the Servant of the Slave.*

*I would like to express special thanks to the following people:
Elizabeth and John Sherrill for their inspiration and
Elizabeth's excellent teaching and also to the class at the Writer's
Seminar in Kolding, Denmark.*

There are *Thinking Further* questions at the end of the book.
All answers can be found within the relevant chapters.

Contents

The End 7

Fight, Fight, Fight! 9

Gossips and Bad News 15

Wishart Street 23

Africa, Canoes and Calabar 27

Mary's First Day 31

On the Street 35

A New Baby and a New Life 39

A Tea Party and a Bully 45

One Tiny Missionary 53

Ready for Anything 63

Treks and Tree Climbing 71

Alarm Bells and Supper 77

Malaria and a Journey 83

A Midnight Adventure 89

Double Trouble 99

Boiling Oil 107

Mary Meets her Match 119

Romance at Last? 123

Back on Track 137

Plague 143

Hippos and Cannibals 149

The Beginning 163

Thinking Further Topics 172

Facts on Nigeria....................................182

Mary Slessor: Life Summary 184

Mary Slessor Time Line...........................185

The End

The steaming, humid night slowly seeped away, defeated by another African morning. Mist rose from the depths of the earth as the sun began its crawl to the top of the sky. Fires were lit and doors opened. The tribes of Calabar were awake.

Some young women, their tightly curled black hair damp with sweat, stood, waiting. A faint whisper wafted through the door of a wooden, mud-floored, hut.

'O Abassi, sana mi yok.' 'O God release me.'

Some hurried movements were heard behind the wooden partition door and finally a long sigh.

The women outside the hut turned to each other. Had it happened? Had she finally left them? Someone stepped onto the veranda to announce, 'Ma is gone.' Gasps of pain and disbelief rippled through the small crowd. A little African boy, scruffy, dirty and chasing a chicken rushed off in another direction, anxious to be the first to tell the other villages, 'Ma is dead.'

Visitors came and went from the rickety wooden hut, clicking their tongues and sighing, deeply, 'What will we do without her?'

As some of the village women discussed the details of the funeral and burial arrangements others sat silently with tear-stained faces. Young women and men who owed their very lives to this woman, to 'Ma', wanted to remember her, to wonder at the young girl with hair like fire who had made such a difference to their lives.

Everyone had their own memory of Ma. As the morning wore on the people shared their memories of this amazing woman.

A little girl with hair like tightly coiled springs of black silk sat on the edge of the veranda, swinging her legs and chewing a blade of grass. 'Ma told brilliant stories.'

A puzzled expression crossed the face of a young man, 'I loved the story Ma told about the cold snow that falls bright and white from the sky.' A little boy shivered as he remembered the stories of the faraway countries, the freezing winds, the icy seas.

A woman, with a pile of children at her feet, sighed, 'I had never heard of love until she came. It was Ma who told me about God, about true freedom. She never lorded it over you like some of the other whites. Ma was different. She was one of us.'

An old grandmother chuckled as she heaved herself up from her seat by the veranda steps, 'Ma was a wonder... but her temper...' everyone laughed. 'Eeh! Even chiefs trembled!'

Fight! Fight! Fight!

'What did you call me?' The sharp scream cut through the cold Aberdeen morning, piercing eardrums and shattering the general chatter in the school yard. Mary was not having any of it. Thin, wiry and quick on her feet she turned to stare eyeball to eyeball with her accuser – a black haired, skinny little fellow with a cheeky grin. 'What did you call me?' she screamed once more.

'I called you a filthy dirty stinker,' he replied, smirking mischievously, 'and so you are,' he added. Mary's bright red hair almost bristled in indignation at the brazen cheek of the little scamp.

'You have nae right to call me anything... you've nae right to call me a stinker.'

'I have too,' piped up the little ruffian. 'I saw your da' last night, wobbling home.' The boy's impression of a drunken walk set the whole class laughing. The steely blue eyes of Mary bored through her enemy's skull. Someone called out, 'You're for it now, man! Mad Mary's going to have you!' The cocky look changed to one of pure fright as the redhead's fist came shooting out of nowhere, laying the young boy flat on the ground.

'Fight, Fight, Fight!' The calls went up and soon every child in the school had thronged round the little redhead and her adversary. They all knew what Mad Mary was capable of or Fire as some of them preferred to call her. One young girl tugged at Mary's sleeve. 'Leave him, Mary. Sticks and stones might break your bones but names will never hurt you. Don't take any notice. That fibber is always calling someone's pa a drunk.'

But the pleas fell on deaf ears and soon Mary was in the thick of tearing hair and kicking shins. The fight was wild but then the headmaster's voice boomed from the other side of the yard.

A big lump throbbed above Mary's left eye and, unable to bear the thought of laughing classmates, Mary ran out of school. The beach beckoned and away she went. Mary cried as she ran, 'None of them really know. None of them really know what goes on, I hope.'

They certainly didn't know the extent of Mary's problems. Many men in Mary's street got drunk. But not every night. Mary's dad did. They didn't go to the pub and spend all their wages instead of bringing it home. Mary's dad did. They didn't hit their wives and children. Mary's dad did.

Other children didn't have to hide bruises behind tattered old rags. Mary did. Other children didn't have to listen to their mother's muffled screams behind the curtain as she tried to defend herself. Mary did. This was Mary's dreadful secret.

Fighting against the wind, Mary found her way out of the city to where the smell of the briny sea stung her nostrils, and the tip of her tongue tingled with the sensation of salt. As Mary finally reached the beach she gazed in rapture at the white horses rampaging along the coast line, leaping and prancing. The excitement caught in her throat as she joined in, racing the boiling waves one after the other. The small craft, moored in the harbour, bobbed up and down frantically. The beach was like a cauldron of nature. Mary thrilled to be in the middle of it. What did it matter if her feet got wet ... they would get dry. To give herself a chance to catch her breath she wandered aimlessly along and dreamed about lots of things. Her eye spotted a beautifully coloured mussel shell, all midnight blue and sparkly. Picking up the shell she remembered the times she had gone shell hunting with her brother Robert.

'Robert.' The name still made her want to cry. His death was still painful. 'Why did he have to die? He was my big brother. He was going to be the missionary that Ma wanted so much. Ma would have been so proud of him but God took him away.'

It was an accusation, Mary was a very angry little girl, but then she remembered something.

'Mother misses Robert more than I do, but she feels differently about it. How is it that she can be so sad and yet so happy at the same time?'

Mary's mother was glad that Robert was in heaven, but Mary just wanted him back here with her picking up shells and driftwood. 'I suppose she is glad he is with Jesus.' However, Mary still wasn't convinced about God. But her mother trusted him and her mother was a good woman. Should she also trust this Jesus like her mother did?

A rogue gust of wind blew sand full in Mary's face. It stung the cut just above her eye and she remembered the jeering classmates and the stinging remarks. It didn't matter how many bruises she got it was always the unkind joke that hurt the most. Though her classmates stood in awe of the tough little redhead, inside was a soft, gentle child.

Mary remembered when it had been better... when her father hadn't drunk so much. But when Robert died it was too much for Mr Slessor. Mary never felt safe around her father again.

But what horrified Mary most was her mother's sobbing at night. 'She thinks I can't hear her when they go to bed. But I do and it's frightening. It would kill Ma if she thought anyone knew what was going on.' Mary stood at the edge of the icy cold ocean. It's chill caught at her heart. She gasped. There was so much she didn't understand and so much that confused her. Yet it still had the power to terrify her. The whimpers from her mother in the night, the frantic and urgent movements as her mother tried to escape the clutches, the grabbing hands, of her husband. Then there was the heavy sound of leather boots thumping and grinding against soft skin. Before Mary was tall enough to reach the top dresser drawer she knew to avoid her father when he had been drinking. Mary was growing up, knowing a lot of things. She knew what a man was capable of when blind drunk. She knew what it was like to see a man and woman live a life of hate and fear together. She knew what it was like to be a child watching it all.

Wiping the sand off her face, Mary flopped over into a dune, made a little nest for herself between some clumps of grass and started to play at school. The unusual thing about Mary's schools was that they always had African children. Her mother's stories about mission work in Africa, particularly Calabar, fuelled Mary's thirst for adventure.

Mary imagined she was a missionary in Africa instead of a schoolgirl by the North Sea. The icy wind and thrashing ocean became a balmy jungle breeze and steaming river. In her imagination her shells became a group of well-behaved little African children. 'Now I will teach you your alphabet... A is for apple, B is for book.' However as soon as Mary's tummy rumbled she announced, 'Well done class, top marks everyone, time to go home.'

As Mary got ready to leave she wondered if she would ever see Africa for herself. 'What would it be like? Mum doesn't think I'll ever be a missionary. She laughed when someone suggested it.' Mary a missionary? With her temper I doubt it!' Ma says missionaries shouldn't have bad tempers.'

Mary sighed, she just couldn't help it. Words would come out of her mouth and into the air before she could catch them. Sometimes she could feel them on the tip of her tongue fighting with her teeth to get out and cause trouble for her. Sometimes she would tie them down inside her throat. More often than not they would just burst out causing havoc. But Mary knew that she didn't help by adding a kick and punch to accompany the words on their way.

As she began the long walk home Mary remembered, 'Ma gets paid today. If she's quick and buys the food before she gets home then there'll be less for Dad to waste down the pub.'

Sneaking in the back door, Mary was careful to avoid the heavy form of her sleeping father. It was after twelve and he was still out cold. 'Must have been a heavy night,' thought Mary… silently shutting it all behind her and skipping out into the yard.

Gossips and Bad News

As Mary sat down to eat a stale piece of bread, two neighbours called out to each other from the back alley. Mary heard her mother's name mentioned and began to eavesdrop on the conversation.

'…She's a lovely woman. We came from the same area before we got married.'

'Really? She's from Old Meldrum?'

'Yes. I knew Mary Mitchell then. It's so sad that her son died. Since Robert's death everything has gone downhill for the Slessors. Mr Slessor is taking it awfully bad. I remember the day that wee redhead of theirs, Mary, was born. 2nd December 1848 it was. That family was young and happy then.'

'I sometimes hear those Slessor bairns making an awful racket. Mr Slessor was really shouting at that young Mary the other night. Did you hear?'

'No, I did not. Was she up to mischief? You know that lassie's a wee terror.'

Mary's face paled. She had prayed that no one would hear her father's drunken shouting.

'Aye. That's true, and they have a big family.'

'Yes, I do pity them. It's a hard life for them.'

Mary's face flushed. She didn't want pity.

'There's not much money coming into that house. Not that there's much money about anywhere these days. But I've heard that Mr Slessor's going to have to leave his job...'

'What? Has he been sacked?'

'My lad works next to him and the foreman's saying that Mr Slessor isn't pulling his weight and keeps coming in late! It couldn't happen at a worse time for them,' Mrs Smith sighed.

Mary's mouth felt dry. Her father was inside, in a drunken stupor, and he was supposed to be at work. This meant that he had lost his job once and for all. The conversation continued.

'How many bairns are there in that family?'

'Let's see... there's Mary, she's the eldest now that Robert's passed on. There's John and Susan and two others, so that makes five in total. Mrs Slessor insists on taking them all to church and Sunday School every week, on her own. Mr Slessor doesn't seem to be the religious type.'

'Yes... there's many a family that could learn a thing or two from Mrs Slessor.'

'You couldn't have said a truer word ... that woman's a saint.'

As she finished off her bread piece Mary wondered how her mother kept going. She smiled as she thought back to one of her very first memories from childhood. 'I was sitting on Ma's knee with Robert at her feet as she read the church magazine to us. It was then that I heard my story of Calabar. Yes, these women are right, I have a very good mother.' Wiping her dirty nose on an old rag, Mary smiled; the day didn't seem quite so bad now.

The gossipers began to wind down their chat with the weather and what was the best cure for warts. Then one gasped, 'Help us, the bairns will be home soon clamouring for food. I'll have to go.'

With that the two women disappeared and Mary decided to meet her younger brother, John, on the way back from school. Mary ran round the corner and bumped into him coming from the other direction.

'Oh, there you are, you big truant! Where did you disappear to? Any news?'

'I think Da' might have lost his job,' gasped Mary.

John's face darkened. He muttered something about jobs being hard to get these days.

'Hmm, I know. But I don't think Da' really cares that much anymore. '

'You could be right, Mary. Ma says that the unemployment is because there's so many people in the city these days. There's not enough jobs for everyone. That's why you see so many starving beggars around. The city just cannot cope with everyone.'

Mary thought about her dad. Would they become beggars if he didn't get a job?

Mary and John hung around at the corner waiting for a sight of Ma coming home with some groceries to fill their stomachs. Smells of homemade baking and the aroma of succulent stew and potatoes wafted out from nearby kitchen windows. Mary longed for some good food. John's stomach rumbled.

As she pictured these families sitting down around their full plates, with pots and pans bubbling away on the stove, Mary knew that if there was anything she could do to help her family, to help her mother make ends meet, she would do it. It didn't matter what.

When Mrs Slessor arrived home she gingerly stepped around her sleeping husband and ushered the children into the yard with a slice of bread and jam. A rare treat. Mary was thrilled, but later that night Mrs Slessor had some news for her.

'Mary love, I've some bad news. Your father's lost his job at the shoemaker's.' Mary didn't tell her about the two neighbours' gossip. 'Your dad's been trying to get work but without success.'

Mary wondered. He certainly hadn't been trying when she saw him sleeping in the kitchen that morning. Mary's mother continued, 'Someone down the pub has said that there might be a job for him…' Mary face burst into a smile before she heard the next bit of the sentence. '… in Dundee.'

Mary's smile vanished. 'Dundee? Dundee? But that's miles away, Ma!'

But then Mary remembered her promise to help her family get back on their feet. It was wrong of her to change her mind so quickly. Creeping into her bed that night she fought the tears and tried desperately to look forward to their new home.

Later Mary gazed out of the window at the moon gazing back at her, its white face was shocked and silent looking. Mary shared, with her brothers and sisters, a bedroom, which was a kitchen and living room during the day. The room off to the side was their parents' room. Hugging her knees against her chest, she wondered when the knocking man would come round. He was the man paid to knock on windows and shout up alleyways to wake everyone up. Every morning, except Sundays, he was there – shouting and hollering and rapping on windows.

Just then Mary heard a drunken song echo down the street. Then she heard her father struggling to keep his balance as he tried to grab hold of the door knob. Susan opened her eyes and peeked fearfully out from under the covers.

'Mary, Is that Da'? Is he drunk again?'

Mary knew who it was without even looking. All three children pretended to sleep as their drunk father stumbled into the kitchen. Mr Slessor grunted at his wife before falling, slumped over the bedroom chair. Mrs Slessor joined her other children in the kitchen. Setting herself up by the stove she wrapped the baby in a shawl and began to pray, softly.

***

The trip to Dundee was uneventful. Sometimes there was even a glimmer of the old Mr Slessor. John and Susan hardly recognised the man. But Mary recognised him. It was like seeing a long lost friend. Mary remembered her father before his drinking took control of his life and before the death of his son, Robert, destroyed him. Genuinely sorry for his behaviour, throughout the whole trip, Mr Slessor tearfully promised to try and do better.

Some days later, two adults, five children and an odd assortment of belongings eventually arrived at their new home – a flat in a tenement building in the city of Dundee. The year was 1859, a year that would be a hard and bitter struggle for the Slessor family. As they entered their new home for the first time 'cold and comfortless' were the words that sprang to Mary's mind.

'Never mind Mary, we'll get it looking nice.' Mrs Slessor tried to be encouraging.

Mary looked at the pile of belongings, which now looked very small, though they had been horrendously heavy to carry. 'Ma, all we have are some pots and pans and some mangy old bedding!'

'Mary, you know we couldn't bring the furniture with us to Dundee, it was too awkward and heavy. Come on now – it's time to get unpacked.'

'That shouldn't take long,' grumbled John.

Dusting and cleaning soon left Mary and the others tired out. Mrs Slessor went to find the toilets. Half an hour later Mary woke from a brief slumber, but there was no sign of her mother and father.

As Mary opened the back door for the first time she grimaced. She couldn't believe the filth of animal and human excrement. Mary's nostrils protested and her stomach heaved. 'Where is Ma? She can't be out in this stench.' She then noticed the outside toilet and heard her mother retching. Mary felt like throwing up herself. Even cows on farms in Aberdeen lived in cleaner stalls than this.

Mary smiled sympathetically at her mother when she eventually came back into the flat. 'It's horrible out there, isn't it, Ma?'

Mary wasn't so sure about Dundee now. There was opportunity here. The jute mills were booming. The material was ideal for making rope, sacking and mats. However, the flats were damp and smelly. And walking the streets was like negotiating your way through a cesspit.

Wishart Street

Mary, John and Susan were all rather thin due to the poor food and tough life they lived. But they soon made friends and started having fun.

The alleys still turned Mary's stomach, but she managed to put that aside just to go out and play with some of the other urchins who ran helter-skelter around the neighbourhood.

'What does your da' do?' asked an inquisitive voice.

'Oh, he was a shoemaker last week but this week he's working in the mills.'

'The mills, eh? He's lucky to get that job. They get higher wages there.'

Mary smiled. She was glad her father had got that job... she hoped he would keep it.

Some things hadn't changed from Aberdeen to Dundee. They still went to church with their mother. Sunday School was still on the agenda at their new church in Wishart Street. The preaching still focused on giving your life to Jesus Christ. However, Mary hadn't done this. 'Why should God be in charge of me?' she wondered. Mary always held something back.

With no school to go to Mary spent most of her time in the back alleys of Dundee, screaming and yelling with the other children, picking fights and throwing stones.

Mary would never be a proper young lady whatever happened. But there was no one better prepared for a life of poverty and hardship than she was. And that was God's plan – though God didn't feature in Mary Slessor's plans at all.

***

Every Sunday the Slessor family, except for Mr Slessor, were to be found in Wishart Street Church.

Mary enjoyed going there and tried not to think about her father digging away in the soil outside their home, 'Pretending he doesn't care a snot about God's day!'

But Mary chose to forget that she had often skipped Sunday School. As a punishment Mrs Slessor would take Mary into the annex, close the curtain and pray for her. Mary felt so bad she wished that her mother would whip her instead.

Sunday meant treats for the Slessor children – a peppermint, a scented handkerchief and wearing your boots. The tight leather pinched your toes a bit but it was so good to show everyone that you had real boots.

As the congregation filed in Mary spent the time in quiet thought, a precious luxury for her.

Tenement life meant very little privacy. However, on God's day and in God's house Mary was free to think and to be alone. Mary knew she didn't feel the same way about God's house as her mother did. She didn't feel the same way about God either.

The other great Sunday treat was the church magazine. It gave reports on what the United Presbyterian churches were doing in the mission field and Calabar. Just then Mary spied someone in the corner holding a copy. Squinting, she tried to get a clearer view of the main heading on the front page. 'Calabar Mission Report.' Mary was ecstatic. 'I can't wait to read it! I hope we get one soon.'

Mary told God about her wish to get a copy of the new magazine and she also tagged on one or two other requests, 'God I want to go back to school again. I want to find out things... to find out about Africa, about the world. I would love to go to Africa one day... If I did I would be really chuffed!'

But Mary would conveniently forget the fact that working as a missionary meant serving God and submitting to him. Mary just wanted the excitement. She knew that Jesus had given his life for her. She would answer all the questions about God's love at Sunday School. But personally it meant nothing to Mary. The answers were in her head not her heart.

As the service drew to a close Mary tried to remember some facts about Calabar. 'It's in South-West Africa and is on the coast, near the equator.' Mary pictured the little map she had once seen during a missionary meeting. Most of it had been written over by this one big word 'Unexplored'.

Africa spread from the southernmost tip of Spain into the Indian Ocean. Dotted lines snaked in and out dividing the massive continent into geographical regions. Most belonged to various European countries… the names told you that… The Belgian Congo, French Equatorial Africa.

The European influence stopped the further you travelled from the coast and the Cross River. The further you travelled the further you went into unknown territory… not many people took the risk.

At eleven years old Mary had no idea that the country she had just been thinking about would one day be her country.

Africa, Canoes and Calabar

Outside church Mrs Slessor called out excitedly to Mary. 'You'll never guess what I've got. The new church magazine!'

'Oh Ma! Can we read it this afternoon?'

'Of course. We'll all read it together. I see there is a big article on Calabar, Mary.'

As they trooped home behind their mother, Susan and Mary chatted about the magazine.

'Where's Calabar, Mary?' asked Susan.

'It's in Africa, on the west coast.'

'Is it far away then?'

John snorted in derision at such a stupid question. 'Of course it's far away! It's Africa, stupid!'

Susan sniffed, 'Well, clever-clogs, how far away is Africa?'

John blushed, not sure if Africa was near France or Germany. Mary then filled them both in on a few Calabar facts. 'Africa is far away and quite inaccessible. Missionaries have a hard time getting around there as they have to travel in the same way as the natives… on foot or by canoe.'

Mary saw Susan's face wrinkle in confusion and she guessed she would have to explain what a canoe was. 'It's a long thin boat that the natives use to travel up and down the rivers. A big river cuts through Calabar. It's called the Cross River. Most of the well-known towns and villages are found dotted along it. The rest of the country is totally unexplored and you have to fight your way through dense forest and jungle to get anywhere. The weather is also hot and stuffy. This is because Calabar is very near the equator.'

'What's the equator?' asked John. Mary tried to remember from her school lessons what the equator was. 'Well it's the middle of the earth. Do you remember the big globe, John, that used to be in the school in Aberdeen?' John nodded. 'The equator is the long line that splits the globe around the middle. All the areas around the equator get a lot of sun so they are very hot. Scotland is further away from the equator so we are colder.'

Susan had one more question. 'Why do missionaries travel like the Africans? Don't they have carriages to take them places? I thought missionaries were very important people.'

'They are, Susan, but being a missionary is a hard life. It is very exciting and thrilling. But there are no roads or carriages in Calabar.'

Mrs Slessor added her own opinion. 'But, Mary, missionaries don't go to Africa for adventures. They go to tell people about Jesus. And as well as travelling like the natives they live like them too.'

'What!' John was astounded. 'Live in huts, cook over fires, wash in rivers? That sounds great!'

Susan wrinkled her nose. Mary's mother smiled. But then Mary went on to describe the other horrors of Calabar… 'There's awful insects living in Calabar! It's because of the swamps. Insects like warm, damp places so Calabar has swarms of insects which bite and make you really sick and then…'

A warning glance from Mrs Slessor stopped Mary in her tracks. It might give John and Susan bad dreams if they heard all about the cannibal tribes of Calabar who murdered their enemies and ate them. As Mary thought about it she realised that Calabar must be an awful country to live in.

Mary had heard of Jamaican slaves who had been set free. Instead of living in safety in foreign countries the slaves had decided to return to the land of their birth, to Calabar, to tell others about the one true God and the Lord Jesus Christ.

As they came to the top of their street Mary shivered at the thought of that frightening country – Calabar. But when she looked around her at the squalid dung heaps, the rotting waste, the squabbling families, poverty and beggars she wondered whether Dundee wasn't as bad as Calabar in some ways. Mary didn't know it then but she was deep in the midst of a training ground. The streets and alleys of Dundee were preparing her. The hunger and squalor of the Scottish slum that she now called home were being used to get her ready for the poverty, squalor and hunger of West Africa. The determination and courage that she had to show to survive on the streets, the ability to hold her own against the roughest urchin, the vilest temper, the gnawing hunger.. they were all qualifications for Africa.

Mary's First Day

Mary's mum had found work as a weaver and Mr Slessor had too. Mary was pleased about this, but what she really wanted was to go back to school.

Every morning Mary saw people going to work at the local mills. In the winter it was pitch black in the morning. The hours were from six a.m. until six p.m. if you were lucky enough to be a full-timer at a mill. You hardly saw the day at all as you struggled to work in the dark and struggled home again in the dark.

The big names in the mill industry made a lot of money. Names like Messrs Baxter Brothers and Company made fortunes for their owners. The mainstay behind these new fortunes was the new power-driven looms which speeded up production. But the reality of Dundee was that it became a mass of miserable humanity. Thousands flocked to the area for work. The Dundee that Mary Slessor came to had over 30,000 inhabitants who all lived in one-room apartments like the Slessors'. That means that more than 30,000 people lived in squalor.

Some months later, Mrs Slessor's deepest fears were realised... the youngest children died...

leaving only Mary, John and Susan. Mr Slessor began drinking again. It was as if the move had all been for nothing. Mr Slessor started to complain about Mary not working at the mills. 'Many a lass is takin' in her fair share.

Mrs Slessor could do nothing about it.

'Mary, I'm sorry. I'll speak to my boss tomorrow. My dream was to see you back in school but we've got to get food on this table somehow.'

Mary sighed… 'Aye Ma, it's alright, I understand.' 'I suppose I'll never get to go to school now,' she whispered to herself. 'Perhaps God doesn't think I am good enough.' But Mrs Slessor came back that evening with a huge smile on her face. 'You start on Monday. And guess what? Since you're so young you'll only be a half-timer.'

Mary looked at her mother's face. 'Ma?' Mary asked, 'Does that mean that I come home for the rest of the time?'

'No, it doesn't,' Mrs Slessor's eyes twinkled. 'All half-timers – children between the ages of ten and thirteen – spend the rest of the time in school.'

'School?' Mary gasped. 'School?'

'Yes. From six to eleven in the morning you work at the mill. From midday to six at night you go to school.'

Mary's smile stretched from ear to ear. Monday couldn't come soon enough. Perhaps God had been listening after all?

Later on Mrs Slessor tucked Mary into bed. Mary hoped and prayed that her father would leave her mother alone tonight. 'If he's too drunk he'll slump in the chair. Then Ma won't get beat up.'

But the faded blue scarf, next morning, didn't quite hide the bruises on Mrs Slessor's neck. Mary said nothing.

'It'll be noisy,' Mrs Slessor informed her daughter. 'You'll find that difficult at first, but soon you'll be able to lip-read what people say.'

'Do lots of people work there, Ma?'

'Oh yes, lots. It's mostly women or children.'

'Why's that then?'

'Well, men are entitled to more wages than women. A woman's wage is half a man's and a child's wage is a quarter of that.'

Mary grimaced at the injustice of it all. Injustice always made her blood boil. It always would.

When Mary entered the mill for the first time she was still shocked at the noise that hit her eardrums. The first hours went past in a whirl of shuttles and looms and instructions and warnings. However, Mary quickly picked up the basics and soon learnt the sign language everyone had adopted. This meant she didn't lose her voice shouting to someone just ten centimetres away from her.

The mill room was long and thin and full of whirring belts and steam-driven pulleys. The weaving-frames clattered with the activity. Life in the mill room was tough. Life in the schoolroom wasn't easy either.

By the time Mary got to school she had already been up for seven hours and had worked like a slave for five of those.

WHACK! Mary leapt out of her skin as the belt came whizzing through the air and crashed down on her knuckles. It was 3.30 in the afternoon and the mathematics problems had been giving her a headache... without knowing it she must have fallen asleep in the middle of class. Rubbing her sore hand she looked up into the icy glare of the schoolmaster. Mary apologised and tried again to focus on the problems. All the energy and life was seeping out of her.

But then, returning from the mill-school at night, she often saw the young men who didn't have a job, who couldn't go to school. They were hanging around the pubs, bitter looking and resentful. It put everything back in perspective. Instead of whining about being tired, Mary was thankful to have a job.

On the Street

Mary still hadn't forgotten her dream of being a missionary. But there wasn't much time to think about it really..

When the knocking man came round shouting and hollering as usual, Mary and her mother would fly about the house waking up the others before joining the thousands of people in the dark morning trek to the mill.

At school in the afternoon it was such a struggle to keep going. When the warm sun came in through the window Mary was often tempted to close her eyes. She wasn't getting the sleep she needed as her father's drinking was getting steadily worse. Mary now refused to leave her mother alone to face him. They never knew when to cook his tea. If he came home early and it wasn't cooked he would fly into a rage... if he came home late and it was burnt or dry he would lash out at his wife for her lack of care.

One night, as he fumbled with the door handle, Mrs Slessor was flustering over a dish of dry fish and potatoes, trying to make it more palatable. Mr Slessor stumbled in, anger already covering his face. Mary stepped forward, 'Leave her be you drunken mess...'

Mary's tirade went on. She must deflect the drunken rage from her mother on to herself. Mr Slessor obliged by punching out at Mary who huddled behind a chair before darting to the other side of the room. 'I've got to get him away from Ma. If we tire him out he'll collapse and forget it all.' However, Mary just wasn't quite quick enough. She fell crashing to the floor – only to be picked up and flung out into the dark.

Mary hid her head in her dirty apron and sobbed. The night drew in and other drunken men groped their way home in the pitch-dark. Someone caught sight of her in the doorway and tried to grab her. She scratched his face and screamed, running blindly down the alleyway.

When the dim morning light appeared, Mary crept out from behind a pile of rubbish. It had been the safest place to sleep. Stretching her neck and rubbing her stiff back Mary wandered home to her worried mother, who burst into tears when she saw Mary.

That night Mrs Slessor sighed. 'We'll have to make another trip to the pawnbroker's. There isn't enough money to pay the bills.'

Mary's mother looked for something that could be taken to the pawnbroker in exchange for money.

The Sunday clothes had been handed over the last time and they hadn't yet made enough money to redeem the clothes back. Mary's mother fondled the wedding ring on her left hand. It was the only item left in the flat that had any value. Mrs Slessor gently placed it in Mary's hand.

'Don't drop it and watch out for the gangs. You'd best go the back way.'

Mary's mother didn't want people to know they were going to the pawnbrokers.

It was shameful for people to see you going there. It showed you up as being a failure.

Once you had handed over your goods the pawnbroker gave a small fee in return.

When Mary handed over the ring for valuation, the broker looked at it critically and handed over a few coins. It wasn't much... but it was money. When she gave the money to her eager mother. She breathed a prayer of thanks, 'Lord, thank you for providing for us once again.'

Mary said, 'Amen.' She meant it too.

A New Baby and a New Life

When Mary was fourteen she became a full-timer at the mills. But the church library gave her the opportunity to read books she couldn't afford to buy, and she devoured them almost as quickly as the Slessor children devoured food. Then Mary's mother announced she was expecting once again.

'Another mouth to feed,' Mary grimaced.

Little Janie Slessor was born in 1862 making the Slessor family six in total.

***

One winter evening Mary was outside with some friends causing mischief, chapping on doors, yelling and shouting. It was one way of keeping warm.

An old woman noticed the girls out in the cold and thought that they might like a seat by her warm fire. She also wanted to tell these girls about Jesus Christ. 'I've got to talk to them about the Saviour. They're running about out there with no care for where they will spend eternity.'

Mary and a few others accepted a seat by the fire and eagerly listened to what the old woman had to say. The meeting became a regular thing, and each week she told them how dangerous it was to ignore God and the love of Jesus Christ.

'You might think you're too young, that you've got your whole life ahead of you. But none of us know when we are going to die. We could die tomorrow. If you haven't asked God to forgive you, death means a lost eternity, hell, not heaven.'

The old woman continued, 'Jesus is the only way to get to God. You only get to heaven if you ask God to forgive your sins in Jesus' name.'

'Sins? What's sins?' someone asked. The old woman explained, 'Sin is anything that doesn't measure up to God's perfect standards. Everyone of us here is a sinner and because of that we deserve punishment. It's only Jesus Christ that can take that punishment away from us.'

'What are the right things to do then? How do we not get punished?' another girl asked.

'Believe in Jesus Christ and ask him to forgive you. You might think that you want to do your own thing, but if you don't have God in charge of your life then you will not spend eternity with Christ. Turn away from your sin and turn to Christ. He longs to save you.

At that point Mary snuggled up to the glowing embers of the fire, quietly dreaming. Then the old woman looked straight into her eyes and gasped, 'Mary, do you not see that fire? Do you not realise how hot it is?'

Mary wondered what the old woman was going on about. Then the old woman did a very unusual and quite frightening thing. She grabbed Mary's hand and brought it up very close to the edge of the hot fire. She felt the smart of the heat on her hand. She winced and the old woman let go.

'Girls,' the woman continued, 'if you were to put your hand into those embers it would hurt you sore! But if you don't turn to Jesus Christ, if you don't ask God to forgive your sins, you will burn in the blazin' fire of hell for ever and ever.'

Mary's face went ashen white. The awful thought of eternal punishment made her feel sick. Running home that night she felt as if the fires of hell were chasing her.

'Where would I spend eternity if I were to die tonight?' she thought. 'What if I walk round a corner and get run over by a team of horses... I'd be a goner and where would I be then?'

That night Mary couldn't sleep a wink. Thinking back to what the old woman had said she remembered the word repentance... turning away from your sin... asking for forgiveness... giving your life to the Lord Jesus. Carefully she crept out from under her blankets and made her peace with God... she asked him to forgive her. 'I am now, I suppose, what the minister calls a child of God,' she thought.

A sigh of relief came from Mary's corner of the mattress and she fell asleep.

The following morning there was the usual chaos as the family tried to find garments and shoes in the pitch-dark.

When all the dressing was over Mary stood alone with her mother. Mary knew that her mother should be the first to know that she had made her peace with God.

Mrs Slessor was delighted to hear Mary's news. 'You won't regret it. God is faithful.' Mrs Slessor encouraged her to read even more. Often they would sit together reading a book that was propped up against the stove. But as Mary struggled on she realised that she was reaching her limits as far as understanding was concerned. The books she was reading, in her breaks from work, were proving more and more difficult.

'Why not go back to school?' suggested her mother.

'Oh, school's for bairns. I'm fifteen years old.'

'Well, Susan is capable of taking on some of your chores. It would be only two nights a week...'

'What? Do you mean that there is school for people my age?' Mary was astonished.

'Yes, evening classes. I know how keen you are to learn, Mary, and I think you should do your best to use the intelligence that God has given you.'

When the term started Mary was one of the new pupils enrolled to do two classes a week.

Then, one night Mary returned home from evening class to find a white-faced Susan holding her arm round the stooped shoulders of her mother. Their father was dead.

Mary wept as she saw his cold body laid on the bed. She remembered the man that he had been... the man that he could have been again if he had only been released from the power of alcohol.

***

Eventually the family moved to a bigger house, with more space, but it was still in the slums. John got a good job as an apprentice to a blacksmith. Susan continued at the mills as a part-timer. Mary slogged on with her lessons. Then one day she read an article about someone she could really identify with... 'Listen to this, Ma, 'Dr David Livingstone, the famous Scottish missionary and explorer is embarking on a new expedition to Lake Tanganyika later this month. Livingstone is an example of the self-educated man. As a young man he worked in the mills but this did not stop him broadening his mind and expanding his education. Livingstone sailed for Africa in 1840 and has since survived many hair-raising adventures including being mauled by a lion. He has travelled hundreds of miles up several rivers and discovered the Victoria Falls on the Zambesi.'

Mary's mother stopped to listen to the account from the church magazine of the pioneer missionary.

'Yes, Mary. He is amazing. Mr Livingstone's belief is that once he has blazed a trail others will follow.'

'Yes,' Mary agreed, 'and he is self-educated, Ma! Self-educated!'

Mrs Slessor nodded. This meant a lot to Mary. Perhaps, though Mary couldn't see it herself, God had a plan to use her to serve him, to serve others, just like Livingstone.

A Tea Party and a Bully

The congregation at Wishart Street was buzzing with excitement. The new minister, Mr Logie, would be preaching this morning. Mary sat beside her mother, blue eyes sparkling. She had high hopes for this new minister and his wife.

'There's so much we could be doing for the poor of Dundee. We have to show them Christ's love in a meaningful way.'

After the congregation milled out on to the street to discuss the new minister, Susan and Mary rushed home to see how John was. His cough was getting worse and they were all worried about his health. However, he struggled on and soon Mary allowed herself to think that perhaps he would pull through.

Eventually Mary was asked to take a Sunday School class and attend the first teachers' meeting at the minister's house. She arrived at the house and shyly rang the doorbell. Mary was dumbstruck at the opulence of the place. Windows were everywhere. Pictures hung in every corner. There were even polished wooden floors and carpeted hallways.

Mary sat in a walnut chair with a red velvet cushion. When the tea and biscuits were handed round Mary was sure she'd drop her cup and saucer.'

Mary was shown round the house. The bedrooms were large and beautifully furnished. The best room, however, was the library. Books were stacked in shelves from floor to ceiling.

When Mary's first official meeting was over she breathed a sigh of relief. Over the next year the minister and his wife became good friends and began to introduce Mary to the strange ways of the middle class. Mary never lost sight, however, that it was the people of the tenements who were her real people.

One day Mary even got her photograph taken. She stood, stiff and proper, in a voluminous skirt, her tight corseted waist looking rather uncomfortable.

But if you wanted to see the real Mary you didn't look at a photograph, you had to see her in Sunday School reading a story or taking the children on a country ramble. Often she would get strange looks as she ran to the other end of a field, squealing with delight and raising her skirts above her knees. She wasn't your usual Sunday School teacher. Then one night the Wishart Street congregation were advised to travel to church in groups as some of the gangs in the area had been causing problems. However, Mary made her own way to the meeting. That was when the gang of youths surrounded her.

'Ah look, a missionary on her way to church.'

Mary smiled. 'Aye, I'm looking forward to it too. We're going to have a grand time.'

The ringleader smirked as he handled a heavy lead weight attached to a string.

'A grand time with your grand friends with their grand cups of tea and enjoying their grand chats…' as he went on he flung the lead weight up into the air and spun it round his head in a circle. He had a particularly threatening look on his face.

Mary saw the lead weight and knew this young man could knock her flat with it. She decided to strike a deal with him.

'I dare you to swing that weight as close to my face as you like. If I stand up to the swinging weight without flinching you have to agree to come with me to church, and on top of that you have to promise to behave!'

The young man smirked, certain of victory, and agreed that if Mary didn't flinch they would all come to her meeting and they would behave. He began to swing the weight. It got closer and closer, four feet, three feet, two feet… Mary never flinched. The boys' eyes widened. Sweat trickled off the ringleader's brow. Two feet, one and a half, one foot. The weight was whizzing just inches from Mary's face but she never batted an eyelid.

Eventually the young man patted Mary on the back, 'Aye boys, she's game,' he said grudgingly. And with that Mary ushered them into the meeting promising them a good time.

Mary's talk had everyone in tears of laughter, including the lads. She had a talent for public speaking. As she said goodbye to them she asked if they would be willing to help her with her Sunday School rambles. 'I could do with some strong lads like you to keep the younger boys in check. We also need help carrying the picnics and things.'

There was a brief discussion and then a unanimous, 'Aye, it'll be grand!'

When the damp cold of winter came back to the grey Dundee streets, John Slessor's cough returned with a vengeance. The family paid for a doctor who diagnosed, 'tuberculosis.'

Mrs Slessor groaned when she heard. Tuberculosis, was a very big killer.

The doctor looked John in the eye and gave him the facts. 'There's not a lot of hope. But if you go to a warmer climate you might recover. It's not certain, but it's your last hope.'

John got a passage to New Zealand. Not long after his arrival, however, the disease got worse. His family received the news that John had died alone in a foreign country. What awful news.

Mary found refuge in God and in her books. It wasn't easy to read in such a noisy, busy, place as the mill room. The flying shuttles and the sheer vibration made Mary's book wobble. She was careful not to let her work suffer, though, which pleased her supervisor.

Mary read early in the morning and again late at night. A small candle lit the desk she had in the room she shared with Janie and Susan. The flame would flicker under Mary's breath as she studied. In the early morning the knocking man would smile as he waved at her in the upstairs window. Late at night the candle would burn until either Janie or Susan mumbled that it was time Mary got some sleep.

One night, as they walked home in the dark, Mary spoke to Susan about God's plans for her life. 'I've been thinking about mission work. Every time I think about it I always come back to Calabar... but I don't know if I should become a missionary. First it was to be Robert, then John.'

Susan piped up, 'Don't be a missionary because Robert and John died. God must call you. It's between you and him. Leave Robert, John and Mother out of it.'

Mary nodded and thanked Susan for her advice. 'I'm almost sure that God wants me to be a missionary. I just have to be absolutely certain.'

Mary went to ask advice of the old woman who had placed her hand so near the fire all those years ago.

'I can't stay long,' Mary said. 'I've come to ask you a question.'

'A question? Very well then Mary ask away.'

'Should a woman like me go to a far-off country to do missionary work among the savages?'

The old woman thought for a moment and then replied, 'Pray and be silent lassie. Listen hard for God's answer.'

Mary knew this was wise advice and gave her old friend a kiss on the cheek before leaving. There was another person she needed to ask... and she knew just where to find him. She made her way to a back alley. 'He won't be far from here,' she thought. She asked around and soon found where he was hanging out. He didn't have a lead weight in his hand this time.

'What are you doing round here, Miss Slessor?'

'I've come to ask your advice.'

The young man laughed and told Mary to fire away. If he knew the answer he would give it to her.

'What do you think of a woman like me going to a far-off country to do work among the savages?'

'Ooh, that's an important question that is.' He thought hard, wrinkling up his brow in the effort. 'Well, I pity these poor 'savages' as they call them. They're like you and me and it's a shame that no one's telling them about God. I needed telling. They do too. Anyway, I can't see anyone stopping you.'

Other people weren't so encouraging. People at church warned her about the dangers of malaria, the mystery disease that struck everyone in the tropics but no one knew why.

That night Mary asked God to show her if he wanted her to stay in Dundee and work for him there or to go to work for him in another country.

That night she dreamt about working in Dundee amongst the poor. It gave her a warm feeling in her heart. Then she dreamt about working for the Lord in Asia. It gave her a warm feeling too. Then the dream of the foreign mission field took on a new focus for her.

She saw a small child, with dark skin, running towards her with tears streaming down her face. In her dream Mary bent down and bundled up the little girl in her arms. The joy she felt was like nothing she had ever felt before. She knew she was called to Africa, but what part?

As she came down the stairs the next morning her mother said, 'You must go to Calabar.'

'Mother!'

'You've been avoiding it, Mary. I don't want a daughter who refuses to work for the Lord just to spare her mother's feelings. I don't want you worrying about me. I want you to obey.'

Later, Mr Logie assured Mary that should she go to the foreign mission field, the Mission Board would see that her family were well provided for.

'So it's forward, Mr Logie?'

'I think so, Miss Slessor.'

Mary gulped and then put things in motion. The year was 1875 and her mother was delighted. Mary applied to the Foreign Mission Board to work anywhere they wanted. Why did she do this when both she and her mother felt that she was called to Calabar? Mary wanted to make sure it was God's will for her, and not some childish dream of adventure. 'I realise, God, that you must decide where I should go. Now I will know for sure your will for me.'

Mary was asked to return to the Foreign Mission Board. As she sat, nervously twiddling her thumbs, a dark suited gentlemen came into the waiting-room to usher her in to meet with the Board.

'Miss Slessor,' a deep voice sounded out from behind a desk. 'Your application has come at a very opportune time. Just this week we have received urgent requests to send teachers out to the area of Calabar.'

If Mary hadn't been dumbstruck she would have squealed for pure joy.

'Calabar! Lord Jesus! Calabar!'

One Tiny Missionary

In 1876 Mary was sent to Edinburgh for a four month course. After that she would sail for Calabar.

She left Dundee for Edinburgh, a city that she found fascinating with its castle, large streets and expensive shops. Princes Street was a wonder. But soon Mary's lessons took precedence over her sightseeing, and she knuckled down to work. It was tough!

'Look at all these assignments! Mary marvelled. Find out about the social and economic condition of Calabar. Discuss the different tribes in Calabar and their different social groupings. Then there's the Efik language lessons!

'You see, Miss Slessor, the Calabar language, the language of the Efik tribe, is largely a tonal language,' her teacher explained. Mary looked blank. What did he mean?

'What I mean is that there are a lot of words that totally change their meanings with a subtle change in tone or sound. You will probably make very stupid mistakes initially. For instance, whether you say a word with a low, medium or high tone can change the meaning of the word dramatically. There is the word for chicken – you say that with a low tone, then the same word said in a medium tone means millstone, and again the same word said in a high tone means knife! Confusing, isn't it!' exclaimed Mary's teacher.

'Fascinating!' thought Mary.

Mary also learned about the palm oil trade. This oil was a good source of machine oil and was crushed out of the bright red palm fruits. One tree could yield 600 lbs or more… but Mary's teacher pointed out that a high yield could only be achieved if the natives didn't drain the sap from the tree to make their own wine. 'This is why the British traders see it as profitable for them to provide the native population with gin and rum.'

Mary's face paled. She knew the dangers of both these drinks.

Then she learned more about the Efik tribe itself. They had a history of being middle men between the British and the inland tribes of Okoyong, Ibo and Ibibio. All the tribes were made up of two levels of society – freemen and slaves. Mary shivered as she heard about the secret organisation of freemen called Egbos who were in charge of brutal justice. The punishments were often violent and harsh.

It hardly seemed any time before it was Mary's last visit home before leaving. Mary held her mother's hand and waited. She listened for the footsteps of the other missionaries who were to escort her to Liverpool. She was soon going to sail to a foreign land. At last the childhood adventure was going to be real. She was so excited but the real joy was the purpose behind it all.

She remembered the dreams and make-believe of long ago – Sitting on a blustery beach, the salt spray tingling her lips, the breakers crashing in her ears and the sea shells, her pretend African children. They would now be replaced by real live ones. She was anxious to hold them, love them, protect them and teach them about their loving, heavenly Father.

Then footsteps were heard on the pathway and Susan and Janie's eyes filled with tears.

'Pray for me,' Mary gasped, as she held onto her mother before exiting out the door.

She arrived on the Liverpool dockside, Mary hugged herself. It was chilly, damp and lonely. She looked at all the barrels and cargo being loaded onto *The Ethiopia*, the ship that would be her home for four weeks or more. A further chill trickled down her spine. She swallowed the tears that threatened to choke her. Barrel upon barrel of gin and rum were being loaded on board the same ship that was to take her to Calabar.

'Lord, help us,' she gasped. 'All that sinfulness and just one tiny missionary!'

The tiny missionary, just weeks from her twenty-eighth birthday, sailed from England on August 5th, 1876.

***

As *The Ethiopia* set sail, Mary remembered the friends and church members who had tried to persuade her to stay.

'What about the cannibals?' one asked her.

'Then there's the wild animals,' voiced another.

'... and the natives there worship the devil!'

Mary had said, 'If it's the post of danger then surely also it's the post of honour.' Mary knew that she was putting her life at risk travelling to Calabar but she knew that it was in obedience to God.

However, as the ship left the sheltered waters of the harbour for the Irish Sea, Mary wondered how well prepared she was for this mission. Would the months of theological lessons prepare her for the practical side of survival in an African country? 'Perhaps I would have been better to have taken lessons in carpentry?', she wondered, as the first waves hit the prow of the boat.

Mary's next concern was more immediate. She felt the first pangs of seasickness as the Irish Sea started to churn her insides. Several times Mary threw up over the side of the boat.

Retreating to her cabin to see if a lie-down would help her heaving stomach, Mary took a brief look at her surroundings. Her cabin was small and compact but as far as Mary was concerned she had never had such luxury. However, Mary's sickness didn't get better but only got worse. She felt miserable as the waves rolled and plummeted along with her insides. Not even the fresh air could get rid of the sick taste from her mouth. Thankfully after the cliffs of home were a faded watermark on the horizon the sickness eased and Mary relaxed.

Taking out her journal she jotted down various points of interest about her sailing companions, the ship itself and the journey she was undertaking.

'The ship is fascinating. I've never been on anything bigger than a ferry before. The SS Ethiopia is a steamship but with the option of sails which we are using right now. The captain says that we shall save the steam power for the headwinds and strong river currents, which we will have to negotiate later on. The entire trip is a journey of 5,000 miles. The captain assures me that we are making a good speed of about 10 miles per hour.'

When they arrived at the Bay of Biscay another storm picked up. Mary, not wanting to spend any more time than she had to in her cabin, sheltered on deck. She saw the massive waves and felt their power as the ship was heaved up and then left to fall again. It was an exhilarating experience. A deck officer jovially asked her whether she thought they would sink this time.

'Naa,' Mary laughed. 'God wouldnae send me all this way just to drown in your silly old ship!'

One morning, Mary was on deck staring at the beautiful blue-green ocean. The colour was inspiring. She never tired of it. Gentle waves washed the sides of the boat as the warm trade winds caressed the canvas sails. A voice sounded out from the crows nest above her, 'Land Ahoy!' Mary strained her eyes in the direction of the deck officer's pointing hand and saw in the distance a glimmer on the horizon. 'Cape Verde,' explained one of the deckhands. 'It's the westernmost point of Africa, the site of the city of Dakar. But we're not stopping there.'

Mary didn't mind, as she was thrilled at her first sight of Africa. The blazing sun above her, the crisp, blue sky – it was a moment to remember.

Soon they changed course to sail eastwards. The smells on the air changed too. As well as the usual salty smell there was an unidentifiable aroma of spice. Then the massive green mountain of Sierra Leone appeared from the depths of the ocean.

Mary looked and looked as they drew closer to the island. Soon she spotted little white houses on the mountainside and the native boats approaching.

Each boat contained several brightly clothed Africans peddling wares of all descriptions.

Mary's first step on African soil didn't take place until several days later when they arrived at Bonny. There she was accompanied on shore by one of the crew members. Walking round the market, Mary was introduced to some of the stranger items on sale.

'You won't be eating any of this stuff, Miss Slessor. You're a nice English lady.'

Mary let the 'English' description pass, but she made a point of putting on a very heavy Scottish accent when next she asked a question.

'Please sir, will ye nae tell me whit that is?' Mary asked, pointing at a pile of strange looking orange tubers in a basket.

'That's yams. The basket beside it has manioc in it, and the next one cocoyams. But, as I said, Miss Slessor, you won't be eating this stuff.'

Mary didn't let on that she planned to eat just like the natives as soon as she could arrange it. She then turned to take a look at another market stall and almost jumped out of her skin in fright. A huge lizard crawled out from underneath the stall. 'Help us! What is that!'

The huge lizard must have been about seven foot long and seemed to be walking wherever it pleased. No one else appeared to want to stop it at all. Mary shivered at the sight of the horrible thing.

'Don't mind that, Miss Slessor. You'll see worse than that before you're through in Africa. That's a monitor lizard. People here worship them so it just goes wherever it pleases. Before long you'll be seeing crocs ten times that size... just you wait.'

The ship continued to sail past villages and settlements. In the distance Mary saw huts with smoke rising from cooking-fires. She wondered about the inhabitants. Were they civilized, had they been reached yet? Then a sailor pointed at the skeleton of an abandoned ship. 'The men on that ship didn't survive. They were eaten.'

Mary's heart sank. The land of Calabar was so much more than yams and manioc and monitor lizards. There was a really sinister atmosphere. The country seeped with evil.

That afternoon, when Mary sat out on deck enjoying a cool breeze, one of the sailors nudged her on the shoulder, 'Take a look at this, Miss!'

Mary got up from her seat and stared at the river bank. She couldn't believe her eyes. 'Now that's a crocodile, Miss Slessor. Must be about twenty feet in length and half a ton in weight. The way he's lying there sunning himself you'd think he was the laziest, slowest, most cumbersome beast around, wouldn't you, Miss Slessor?'

Mary agreed.

'Well, you're wrong. Those little legs don't look up to much but I've seen a croc move before… and they can move like lightning.'

Mary's face went a little pale. In her imagination she could tackle warrior chiefs and stubborn natives. But what would she do against a crocodile?

The following day Mary realised that very shortly she would be at her final destination. As she sat in her cabin packing, she felt the ship change direction and she ran up on deck to check what had happened.

'We've reached Seven Fathom Point and have left the Cross River. Just another five miles now.'

The Captain was right. Five miles later the ship turned a corner and there was the anchorage of Old Calabar. Mary heard the screeching animals, squawking birds and laughing, excited children on the jetty.

Then Mary spotted the welcome committee in a native canoe. She heard the rhythmic chanting of the native boatsmen as they swung the oars into the water and heaved out into midstream. Their muscles shone, the drum beat in time to the stroke. The boatsmen wore bright red hats and dark loin cloths. On board a European man waved excitedly at Mary. She waved back. Mary inspected him. He looked slightly out of place with his white, pressed, suit, dark-blue tie and well-groomed moustache. The white suited gentleman grinned widely, oblivious to Mary's scrutiny.

As the canoe reached the side of the boat, a ladder was lowered for Mary to disembark. Mary breathed a sigh of relief. She'd arrived. She was here. '…and I know you are here with me God. I can feel you. I can sense you, protecting me, comforting me. You will always be with me.' Then strong, dark, hands reached out to steady her as she clambered down. Shining black eyes twinkled at her as they helped her. Mary felt very welcome. 'So this is Africa,' she said, somewhat naively.

It was 11th September, 1876.

Ready for Anything

Mary marvelled at the welcome she received on the jetty. Duke Town was in the distance and a whole crowd of inhabitants had come to welcome the new missionary.

The children from the mission school formed a guard of honour to escort Mary on shore. Then, for the first time since her arrival in Africa, Mary smelt the strong, potent smell of palm oil. Her nose twitched and the white-suited man nodded and said, 'The palm oil, that's what you're smelling. It will take some getting used to.'

'Yes,' Mary said, wrinkling her nose. 'It's used for engine oil, isn't it?'

'Yes, and soap and candles, too. The woman waving at you there is Mrs Sutherland. You'll like her.'

'Miss Slessor, it is a delight to see you! Mr Sutherland exclaimed. We have been waiting for your arrival for so long. Let's walk up the road together and get to know each other.'

Arm in arm the novice and the experienced missionary strolled towards Duke Town. Calabar's past and its future were condensed in two women.

***

The unloading of the luggage was quickly organised. People came out from all corners to greet, and gawp at, the new missionary or 'Ma Akamba' (White Ma) as some of the local residents called the white women missionaries. Mary smiled at the staring faces and curious looks; it was peculiar to attract so much attention but she would get used to it, eventually. As Mrs Sutherland went into the schoolroom to supervise the cleaning up of blackboards and desks, some other missionaries pointed out one or two points of interest in the town.

'The mission house is at the top of the hill because you get a breeze. You can see Duke Town from the house. Two miles beyond Duke Town, along the Calabar River, there's Old Town and directly opposite us, across the river here, is Creek Town. There's a mission station there too so on clear days we can actually send messages to each other by semaphore.'

Mary laughed at that. 'What an ingenious idea! Could you tell me a bit more about Mrs Sutherland? She is fascinating.

'I know what you mean,' a young man replied. 'There is something about her. She's normal, yet very unique. Quiet, but very stern when she needs to be. Once there was a battle between two nearby towns. Mrs Sutherland heard about it. She arrived to find the victorious side setting light to the huts of the defeated side, with the women and children inside them. Mrs Sutherland went straight into the flames and smoke to save as many lives as she could. White traders finally arrived to see what they could do, and found Mrs Sutherland trying to free some prisoners by breaking their chains with a gun butt.'

Mary's astonished face said it all.

When Mrs Sutherland rejoined them Mary looked up to her even more. This was the sort of missionary she wanted to be – strong, fearless and effective!

As they continued to walk on up the hill, Mary remembered Susan's first inquisitive questions about missionary life. 'Why don't the missionaries have carriages?' The roads were pretty rough round about Duke Town so that was why there were no carriages. But Mary was curious about why she hadn't seen any horses or donkeys.

That question was soon answered, 'The tsetse fly killed them all. Missionaries and white traders took some horses, mules and donkeys here in the first few years, but none of them lasted. The bites drive them mad and then kill them off.'

'So all journeys are done on foot then.' Mary smiled, trying not to think of how hot she was already. Her European clothing dragged her down.

Mary sweated under frilly underwear, a heavy skirt, hat and gloves.

'Yes, except when we travel on the river,' Mrs Sutherland said sympathetically. 'All luggage is carried on the head, as these men are carrying your luggage now – or on canoe. By the way, please don't go off on your own anywhere. If one of the missionary staff can't go with you, then you can always get two or three boatmen to go.'

Mary realised that Mrs Sutherland was telling her this for her own good, but she felt like a child being told what she could and couldn't do. Surely Mrs Sutherland realised that she wasn't just here to hide away in the mission school. Mary wanted to reach out, beyond the safety zone to where the people had never heard the truth about Jesus Christ.

Later, Mary was introduced to her duties in the school and dispensary. She learnt the basics of dispensing medicine, which would prove valuable to her in later years. She also learnt about the local tribes and their customs. There was a lot to learn. For example, there were the Okoyong tribes – the arch enemies to the Efik tribe. Then there was the Aro tribe who had all the other Calabar tribes under their thumb because of their god, Chuku. They offered sacrifices of slaves to it. Mary ached to destroy this stranglehold that evil had over these people. She knew the only answer was Jesus Christ.

The mission had, however, discouraged further development into the unknown territory. The risk was too high and the results nonexistent. The Efik tribe did not want missionaries exploring the Okoyong territories either. They were afraid it would threaten their control of the trade routes.

Mary's faith in God didn't allow her to be faint-hearted. 'It's not right sitting around worrying if I'm allowed to do this or that,' she fretted. 'Surely we should focus on what we can do and just do it?'

Mary didn't want to retreat, or even stop to take stock of things; she always wanted to press forward. But for now she had so much to learn she kept her head down and did her best to grasp the basics.

Mary soon made friends at the mission and amongst the local Duke Town residents. The mission staff totalled thirteen people, including Mary. Quite a few staff were Jamaican. This was because the very first people who had a burden for Calabar were the slaves who had been forcibly removed from the country many years before.

Although they had been horrendously treated, many discovered the good news of Jesus Christ. Their first thought when slavery was abolished in Jamaica, was to bring the good news of Jesus Christ back to their homeland.

Mary asked Mrs Sutherland one day, 'How do we persuade the Africans that Christ loves them when it was white people who put their families into slavery? For most of them their only memories of people of our colour have been negative ones.'

Mrs Sutherland agreed. 'You're right, Mary. What's more they look on Christ as the 'white man's god' and are confused when they see white men disobeying God every day. We tell them one thing at the mission, yet they see other white people disobeying God's rules.'

'We have so much work to do,' sighed Mary

'Yes,' Mrs Sutherland exclaimed. 'We have to get them to see past our skin. Being white is a disadvantage to telling people about Jesus in this country. We need a key to unlock this situation. I've prayed that God will send us help, that he will break down these doors for us.'

But God already had the solution to this problem. God would use Mary. She would take Christ to the captives. He would set them free.

However, Mary was anxious to be set loose in Duke Town. The mission wasn't stretching her enough. Mary made up her mind that as soon as she could she would start doing a real missionary's job. She'd been cooped up far too long already. Grumbling slightly, Mary made her views known.

Mrs Sutherland smiled. 'We're not trying to keep you cooped up, my dear. It's only your health we're concerned about. If you do too much at first your body won't be able to cope with it.'

'I know that, Mrs Sutherland. It's just that I want to do more than measure out medicine.'

'You will, Mary, you will. But acclimatize first. I know you're anxious to get going. Next week we will arrange visits to the local Christians and, as you get a better grasp of the language, you can visit the women's compounds.'

Mary was relieved and soon with Mrs Sutherland, she made her first excursion into Duke Town.

As they walked through the muddy, humid, streets, Mary poured sweat. Mary wished that she could take off her boots and go barefoot like the children. 'Like I used to do in Dundee.' Mary smiled, remembering.

Mrs Sutherland pointed out the huts. 'Each hut is built around interconnecting yards. The walls inside are decorated by hand by the women. They use vibrant colours, and paint whole walls with jungle scenes. The backs of the huts face the road. If you want to enter you have to go into the yards. The entrances face away from the main road.'

'For safety I suppose?' asked Mary.

'Yes. Safety is a great concern. All entrances are guarded by watchmen. They keep out the human intruders. Charms are hung around to keep out evil spirits. When you gain access to the courtyards you will see shrines are kept in the corner of the main yard.'

'What are the shrines for?'

'To appease ancestors. They offer up gifts of fruit and vegetables or a chicken. In this compound, however, one person comes to church. None of the free women are allowed out without permission. It's a bit ironic. You can be a woman, married and 'free' but have no freedom. And then the slave women can come and go as they please. It's a slave woman who comes to church.'

Mrs Sutherland smiled to the watchman as they entered the yard. She was puzzled at Mary's relaxed reaction. 'You're not like the others, are you?'

'What do you mean?' asked Mary, as they waited to be introduced to some of the women.

'Well, I watched you today. Most new female recruits would have keeled over by this stage. I didn't realise you were so robust!' Mrs Sutherland laughed.

'Oh,' Mary smiled. 'I suppose you mean the smell, dirty people, filthy children. It's just like home, except for the heat.'

As they made their way home, Mrs Sutherland smiled at Mary..

You've done well today. I think you're ready for a little bit more work, my dear.'

Mary breathed contentedly. She was ready! More than ready! She was ready for anything.

Treks and Tree Climbing

A few weeks later Mary was given three crew men to be her guides and protectors as she went on tour to the mission outstations.

'At last I am going to see the real Africa!' exclaimed Mary, delighted.

The mission staff briefed her about wildlife to look out for.

'Watch out for the snakes. Pythons hang from trees and crush their victims to death. Have you heard about the driver ants? They're nasty creatures, about an inch long and vicious. They travel in long columns, about 1,000 in each. And if they come across someone lying in their path, the ants will eat them. If you get bitten by driver ants you've got two options.'

Mary listened intently.

'One, strip all your clothes off or run as quick as you can to the nearest river and plunge in.'

'Right, well, thanks for the warning,' said Mary.

'No problem, and remember nature's not all bites and stings – there's beauty too. Watch out for the butterflies, kingfishers, long legged herons, silver-grey parrots, green doves and then there's the bee eaters. And the flowers and their scent are just so different to anything you will have smelt before.'

As Mary went on her travels she enjoyed all these things and wrote to tell her family back home about all that she was doing.

Dear Mother, Susan and Janie,

As you know I have been doing a bit more travelling lately. The flowers are wonderful. I wish I could send them home to you. I am sure you would love them as much as I do. But I think my favourite must be the monkeys. They have me in stitches — they get up to such silly antics and games. I saw some playing on a vine the other day. Then they began to squabble over a piece of fruit! The racket they made was piercing.

Most of the long trips begin in the morning, very early. I am out of my bed long before the first sun ray. Usually I am not very good in the mornings. It's often a struggle for me to wake up and get moving. However, when there is a trip to go on or an adventure round the corner, I never have any trouble. When I am in the thick of mission work and reaching the tribes with God's word, I am always enthusiastic!

But early morning is something else in Calabar. As I sit in the middle of the canoe the whirls of mist rise up off the river. I gaze in wonder as the red sunrise lights up the forest and the edges of the trees are outlined in a deep scarlet flame. It's beautiful. It's magnificent. It's so strikingly different from the squalor of everyday life in Duke Town.

Being in a canoe doesn't mean, however, that I don't get wet. I have been up to my armpits in water as we have struggled through creeks that the crew men can't row through. I do feel envious of the native women. As the heat rises, I sit on the river bank, sticky and sweaty while they can strip off and jump straight in. Lady missionaries are not allowed to bathe in the river.

Night in the forest is a mystical time, especially when we walk through the tall, stately pillars of trees with their blossoms wafting down like snow from between the branches. There is no vegetation under our feet. This is because the large trees cut off all the sunlight. They keep it all for themselves. Nothing will survive underneath them. The other notable thing is the amazing processions that follow me everywhere I go. White women are still a novelty here. Women and children throng around me, poking me in the side, fingering my flaming red hair, which is such a fascination to them.

The pathways up to the villages are notable in that they always cut through very dense bush. This is primarily for protection. The paths themselves are deep with the pounding of generations of feet.

The currency used in Calabar is thin copper hoops. Mostly people barter with each other, swapping goods that they have with things from someone else that they need or want.

Violence is a prominent part of the culture here. Every village has a clearing where entertainment is held; this includes floggings and executions. On the edge of the clearing is the palaver house, where the chiefs and elders meet to discuss village affairs. Beside the palaver house there is a large drum. It is made out of a hollowed log. They beat it in order to warn the people of danger. The drum is also what they use to call the people back from the fields to hear a special decree by the Egbo — the group of men who make all the laws in these tribes. The drum is also used to warn the people that the Egbo are having a procession nearby. Only the highest village officials can witness an Egbo procession. If you are caught outside when the procession goes by you are flogged.

Even today, the young men gain standing and position in their communities by how many enemy skulls they can collect. The women who go to work in the fields, are constantly guarded by armed sentries. Lookouts are posted in nearby trees.

Right now I am settling back into the mission house. I must confess I am finding it slightly stiff and starchy after the freedom of travel that I have enjoyed over recent weeks.

My next appointment is tomorrow's Sunday afternoon tea party, put on specially for the white traders and *captains. I know already that this is going to be very trying – small talk, chitchat and no real spiritual input. An utter waste of time.'*

Love Mary.

Sunday afternoon lived up to Mary's expectations and she felt like a fish out of water and totally tongue-tied.

As the humid afternoon drew on, Mary sat as close to the window as she could manage in the hope of catching some small breeze. The clinking of tea cups and the sipping of tea and polite conversation almost drove her mad.

Mrs Sutherland gently smiled at Mary squirming in the corner. Mary took a deep breath and smiled back. She loved Mrs Sutherland; she loved all the missionaries and respected them for the great work they were doing. But Mary just wasn't one of them. She didn't fit into their mould. She had been made quite, quite differently.

As the visitors made polite exits, and waved and exclaimed what a wonderful time they had had, Mary gave a sigh of relief. Then she slumped into a comfy seat and scratched her back. How she longed to get out of this blasted corset! Mrs Sutherland came in and patted her on the back.

'Well done, I know it's hard but you're managing. Are you looking forward to teaching the children again?'

Mary smiled genuinely. 'Yes, I am. We're teaching biology and nature studies this term.'

'Yes, I heard that. What a good idea.'

'I think so,' said Mary cheerfully. She was looking forward to the field trips. And next morning Mary was up early, eager to get started.

'Right class, follow me. Our field trip today is an excursion into the bush. We're going to learn together about the nature around us. Quick march!'

With a lot of giggles and excitement the children marched off with their teacher into the bush behind the mission compound. Flowers were pointed out and dissected. Children discovered seeds and other things. Then, safely away from the mission house, Mary yelled, 'Last one to the knobbly tree is a hairy monkey!'

With a scramble a hop and a leap, Mary scaled the tree easily. At the end of the month Mary wrote in a little notebook. 'I have now been up every tree worth climbing within shouting distance of the mission house.'

But very soon things were going to get a little bit awkward for the tree climbing missionary.

Alarm Bells and Supper

William and Louisa Anderson had been on leave and in, January 1877, they were back. Louisa was determined to get that new girl, Mary, in order. 'Running races? Climbing trees? What does she think she is doing?'

Mary's first clash with Louisa happened on the morning that Mary was in charge of the rising bell.

'Och, I've slept in,' Mary mumbled as she opened her eyes. She charged down the corridor in her nightgown and rang the bell frantically. Mrs Anderson, stepped out into the hallway and scolded Mary.

'Most of us are dressed, Miss Slessor. Try to be more punctual tomorrow.'

Mary, determined not to be caught out again, barely slept that night. She eventually dozed off and then woke up in a fluster. Bright light was shining through her window.

'Och no, I've done it again!' she cried in despair as she ran, eyes half-closed, down the corridor. Grabbing the bell she rang it boisterously, waking everyone at three in the morning. In her anxiety not to sleep in, the bright African moonlight had woken Mary. Confused, she thought that she had slept in again. Nobody had a good sleep that night.

Mary eventually got the hang of waking up on time without such a thing as an alarm clock or a knocking man. But Mrs Anderson was still annoyed with Mary's tendency to run races and climb trees with the children. It meant that she was often late for meals.

One afternoon Mary slunk in at the back of the dining room and sidled up to the cook. 'Sorry I'm late.' Just then a polite cough was heard from Louisa Anderson.

'Miss Slessor, it's good to see you at last. Unfortunately meals are served promptly at this mission house. Cook has been given instructions not to serve stragglers.'

Mary had to go to her room, hungry. However several minutes later she heard a quiet knock on the door. A pair of twinkly eyes peeked round the door.

'Oh, Mr Anderson! I am sorry about the bother. I hope Mrs Anderson isn't too angry with me?'

'Oh, not at all. Louisa just likes things to run smoothly. Here's a little supper I smuggled up. If you go climbing trees again, try not to be late!'

But try telling a dog not to bark, or a cat not to chase a mouse.

Mrs Anderson was always ready with her lectures and Mr Anderson with his smuggled snacks. It wasn't until years later that Mary discovered that these snacks were not made by Mr Anderson but actually by Mrs Anderson. She would quietly give them to her husband to smuggle upstairs!

***

Eventually, Mary was given the opportunity to explore Ikonetu and Ikororfiong, two missionary stations she hadn't yet managed to visit. The missionaries she travelled with were great company, telling her about other tribes they had met and dangers they had experienced – just the sort of missionary work Mary felt that she should be doing.

One man had been quite far up the Cross River. 'I actually made contact with the Akunakuna tribe. They are right up the Calabar and then into the interior. Most of the tribes I met were curious to find out more about God and the Bible, except of course the Okoyong.

The Okoyong actually ambushed us, chained us up and carried us off to their village. They demanded a ransom of rum or else they would kill us. We eventually negotiated our release without the ransom, but I'm afraid I had to promise not to travel through their territory again.

I'm thankful our guides weren't Efik tribesmen. If they had been I believe they would have killed us all on the spot. The Efik and the Okoyong are still bitter enemies. The principal pastime of the Okoyong is raiding Efik farms for livestock, women and heads.'

Mary grimaced. She hated the thought of violence. But, when it came to fighting her way through the undergrowth, climbing over a fallen tree and wading through a muddy creek she was in her element.

Mary was overjoyed to meet the women and children from the nearby village. They clamoured round her, gesticulating in what Mary thought was a rather threatening manner until she was assured that they wished to be friendly with her.

When it was time to go, Mary felt her heart wrenched in two. 'These people need someone to tell them about God. But what can we do?' She didn't know.

One afternoon Mary sat, drumming her fingers on the schoolroom table. The pupils were getting nowhere with the sums she had set them. Nobody seemed in the mood for working. Mary sighed. Her mind and heart were all over the place. One minute she was here in Duke Town helping the children with their problems. Then in a matter of minutes her imagination would take her into the deepest interior, to the Okoyong, to the unheard of tribes, hostile, lost and in desperate need of God and his book. But who would risk travelling through Okoyong territory?

The problems seemed insurmountable and it was getting Mary down. As none of the children could concentrate on doing any work, Mary just let them go. They were all boys. She had noticed this before, of course, but it hadn't bothered her unduly. However now it did. Since her return from her last trip things that had mildly annoyed her in the past were really getting under her skin.

Mary wandered down the path to the town, praying and thinking as she went.

'How they treat their women just disgusts me.' Mary couldn't believe the torture of the fattening houses.

The men believed that a truly beautiful woman was a fat one. So, at puberty, when a girl was preparing for marriage, they lock her up in a fattening house. The girl was kept there and fed on special foods. She was not allowed any exercise. Some girls at their wedding feast were so ill and so heavy that they could hardly walk to the feast, let alone stand!

Worse still, some Efik tribeswomen, were chosen to accompany their husband to the other world. Certain wives and slaves were killed and buried along with the husband. The other wives were then shut up in a widows' house. They were not allowed to wash and were soon covered with sores and vermin. The mourning period could go on for years.'

However, what Mary hated most was how the people treated twins. They believed one twin was possessed by a devil and that the mother was a devil worshipper. Both babies were put into large pots and left in the bush to die. The mother, too, was forced to flee for her life.

Mary looked down on the town where she worked. The desire to do something and the frustration of not being able to, was almost eating her alive.

Just then Mrs Sutherland appeared round the corner. 'Ah Mary, just the girl, we're going on a visit to the women's compounds in Duke Town, remember?'

Mary grimaced. She hated these visits now. They accomplished so little. But Mrs Sutherland had a new task for Mary to do.

'I want you to the slave girls today. Only they don't know any English at all. It will be hard work.'

'That's more like it,' thought Mary, and with new vigour she plunged into another job which was part of God's plan for her. As the slave girls knew no English, Mary learnt more Efik. Mary also formed friendships with the girls. She could relate to these girls. She could sympathise with these young women in their poverty and slavery. Mary was relieved, 'This is what I was called to Africa to do.' But God had further plans for Mary. She just had to learn to wait.

Malaria and a Journey

'Mary, how are you getting on with your language learning?' Mr Anderson patted Mary on the shoulder encouragingly and smiled.

Mary sighed. 'It's harder than I thought it would be. I am learning, but it is so slow. I just have so much that I want to be able to tell these slave girls but I can't. My language is still not good enough.'

'Keep going, Mary, keep going. It won't happen overnight, but it will come eventually.' Mary smiled and sighed again as Mr Anderson waved goodbye.

'It is so difficult to wait,' she muttered to herself, drumming her fingers on her knee in frustration. Insects buzzing around her face almost drove her to distraction and she swiped at one. 'Got ya!' With that she quickly cleaned the black board and then marched back up to the mission house. 'I had better find something to do to keep me out of mischief.'

Mary busied herself in the schoolroom, tidying out drawers and giving the place a good clean out. Towards the end of the afternoon Mary began to feel a bit warm. 'It must be all this exercise. Running around and clearing out is harder work than you realise, and the afternoon is quite stuffy, I suppose.'

A drop of sweat trickled down from her forehead. Quickly Mary wiped it away, only to have it replaced by another one and then another. Mary sat down on the chair to steady herself. Her legs felt wobbly, her eyesight hazy and blurred, she felt very peculiar.

Mrs Anderson walked into the schoolroom to give Mary instructions for the following day. She took one look at her and stopped in her tracks. 'Mary!'

Mary felt the heat increasing, her ears buzzed loudly. Mrs Anderson called out as she rushed to help her. Strong arms surrounded her and soft hands felt her forehead. Mr Anderson's diagnosis was 'malaria.'

Mary was immediately taken to bed. Cool, damp, cloths were laid on her head to try and take the fever down. The only medicine known to have any effect on malaria, quinine, was administered. There was nothing much anybody else could do except hope, pray and wait. Mrs Anderson worked day and night, desperate that Mary should pull through. Mary, delirious from the fever, spent hours just babbling words that meant nothing. Sometimes Mary just muttered sounds and grunts. A rota was set up amongst the women to care for her around the clock. Eventually the fever subsided and the recovery began.

Mr and Mrs Anderson breathed a sigh of relief, 'Mary, we're so thankful. We thought you were going to be one of the ones who didn't make it!' And Mary realised how close she had come to death.

'Many of the young women who come out to Africa, full of energy and beauty, come down with malaria. It makes their beauty a memory and their energy is gone for ever.' Mrs Anderson gazed out the window, her eyes vacant, staring. Mary wondered if she was thinking of someone who had died, someone they had prayed for, cared for, but lost?

'If malaria doesn't kill them it ruins them for life. Once you have had it you never totally get rid of it. At some point in the future it will always flare up again.' Mary now knew that her future in Africa would be one of pain and illness. Malaria was now a fact of life.

But, as the weeks went by Mary's energy came back. She was tough, resilient and soon the urge to climb trees was just too strong to fight.

Mrs Anderson seemed to lose her compulsion to re-create the young redhead into a suitable lady missionary – at least as far as climbing trees was concerned. She just looked on with mild disapproval. The fact was that they had nearly lost Mary and everyone, including Mrs Anderson, was just too glad to have her back, hale and hearty. As Mary clawed her way up another tree, grabbing a creeper in her left hand and a branch in the other she smiled; the old cheeky twinkle in her eye was well and truly back.

But the problem that Mary had been warned about came true. The malaria returned, again and again. Her plans to go out into the forests, to meet the real Africa, to reach the unreachable, to bring Jesus Christ to the lost tribes of the Calabar, seemed to be just unobtainable dreams.

Mary had even begun making a strong friendship with the Efik tribal chief, King Eyo. He was a Christian and spoke fluent English and Mary knew that getting alongside people like him could help her in her long term plans to reach into the heart of the jungle. Mary even had grander plans than befriending this local chief.

'Someone needs to reach the Okoyong,' Mary exclaimed one day in the hearing of Mr Anderson.

'What? That bunch of mercenaries?' he sighed. 'Mary, get that thought out of your head this instant. Missionaries with more experience than you have escaped from that tribe, thankful for their lives.'

However, as the months passed by, the idea was even more ludicrous. Mary's health got worse. A letter home says it all. Mary was depressed, discouraged and thoroughly disillusioned.

Early in 1879 she wrote, 'I want my home and my mother.' Mary was homesick. She had one more year to go before she finished her four year tour of duty. She was so broken that the mission decided to send her home early. Mary hadn't even been in Africa three years, and it seemed as if Calabar had chewed her up and spat her out.

The steaming equatorial rivers, the lovely little African pupils, the excitement and adventure she had imagined in her childhood held little fascination for her now. All Mary had wanted to do since the moment she had arrived in Africa was to tell the people of Calabar about the Lord Jesus Christ, her friend and her Saviour. She had wanted to reach out, far and beyond the comfort of the mission house, to go where she was needed. But with her plans thwarted and her enthusiasm quashed, perhaps it wasn't Calabar that was the problem but the very mission where she was supposed to be working.

People had tried to force her into a mould that she wasn't designed for. And, instead of recognising how unique she was, they tried to make Mary like them. They didn't see her potential. Mary must have felt caged. She had discarded the restricting corsets as useless and unnecessary pieces of clothing – but she still felt that the confines of the mission house restricted her in a much more debilitating way.

Mary retreated. She went home for a stay that would last sixteen months in total, much longer than the leave taken by most of the mission staff. As the months passed, many at the mission thought they had seen the last of her. She had come full of energy and vision but she had left tired, crumpled and despondent.

However, intense conversations with Mr Logie, her old minister from Dundee, helped Mary get to the root of her problem. She wrote a letter to the mission board explaining that she had to get out of Duke Town. Mary needed to get into the forests and the people in the forests needed her to come.

Mary then heard that two other missionaries were returning to Calabar shortly. Without clearing it with the mission board, she packed her bags and arranged a passage back to Africa with them. Impulsive, opportunistic, enthusiastic, Mary was ready to get back to work. But was the mission ready for her?

A Midnight Adventure

Were they ready for her? Well, in one way they were, because on arrival Mary received some longed for news.

'Mary, the Old Town station needs opening up again. It's been abandoned for over a year now.' The messenger went on to describe the problems, to try and give Mary a more realistic picture. 'It's in bad need of repair. You're going to be on your own....' But Mary wanted independence. However, wisely, for a first independent charge, Old Town wasn't too far away. The mission would still be able to keep in regular touch with her.

Bursting with ideas and enthusiasm, Mary could hardly wait to get things started. Mary, a young woman in her thirties, had a real vision for this part of Africa.

Unable to wait a moment longer, Mary insisted on helping the Africans refurbish the mission house. The building was designed in the usual way with an upper storey supported on poles. Inside was a room for the missionary, one for the girls, and underneath there was room for a dispensary and a boys' room.

Mary also 'refurbished' herself in a more practical style.

'What is the point of wearing European clothes that only get in the way!' Mary now insisted on simple cotton clothing with no frills. 'And I'm sorry... but that long hair was just getting me all hot and bothered so I chopped it off.' Mary now sported a very neat and tidy bobbed hairdo, which Europeans thought very unfeminine.

Soon Mary could be seen going around her duties wearing a long sleeved billowing gown, no shoes, no hat and her short bob neatly combed into a left side parting. The only other thing she always took with her was an umbrella. Mary found it useful for many things... and was even known to brandish it at the occasional threatening tribesman.

Friends and colleagues from the Creek Town and Duke Town mission stations called in now and again to see how the new missionary progressed. Two deputies arrived from the Foreign Mission Board. One man was a young recruit, while the other was older and more experienced. They had been instructed to make a special visit and were shocked at the amount of work Mary was managing to pack into every twenty-four hours.

As they sat down with her in the missionary room, one deputy rubbed a sore spot on his foot and sighed.

'How do you do it, Miss Slessor? We've hardly stopped all day. I've never had a Sunday like it!'

Mary laughed. She realised that while she had run them off their feet.

At daybreak they had risen to a quick breakfast cooked by one or two African girls. Mary had delegated all the cooking tasks to the girls. They boiled everything and used only local produce. This meant that the cooking was simple and that Mary was free to do other work. It also meant that they saved money.

After breakfast Mary hustled the two deputies out of the house and began the trek through the bush to the small village of Qua.

'I started a school there a few months ago and we have a service here every Lord's day. The classes and services are held under the tree in the good weather and in the palaver house if it's bad.'

'The palaver house?' asked one of the deputies, puzzled. 'What's that?'

'Surely you know what a palaver house is? You're from the Foreign Mission Board! Och well, it's just like a courtroom or meeting house for the local tribes people. All the major discussions and meetings are held there. And all serious decisions are made there. Justice is handed out by the tribal officials.'

On arrival at Qua the deputies got their first view of a palaver house. The clay floors with enemy skulls embedded in the walls was an unusual setting for a Christian service. However, as the weather got worse it was the most sensible option.

After the service was over Mary hustled them on to Akim, where she was to hold another service. Then, Mary and the deputies hurried back to Old Town for the midday Sunday School. In the afternoon they travelled to Ikot Ansa for another service and then returned to Old Town for the evening service. It had been quite a day.

'Phew,' the older deputy stretched out his legs and sighed. 'You're a wonder, Miss Slessor. You run a mission station, take services, look after orphans…'

The younger deputy smiled. 'Oh yes. I forgot about the orphans.'

Mary laughed, 'They're quiet after they go to bed. The babies aren't a problem. If you keep them fed and happy they don't complain too much. I do wish we could do more about the twins' situation however.'

'Yes, I've heard about that. Superstition still has a stranglehold on this country. Anyway, Miss Slessor, I'm for bed. We'll see you in the morning. Sleep well.' Both the deputies yawned, stretched and trundled off to their makeshift bunks.

But Mary wasn't ready for sleep. The thought of the unwanted twins left to die out in the jungle kept her up for hours. Suddenly, just as she was about to fall asleep in her chair a voice whispered at the door to her room.

'Ma Slessor! Come quick. Come quick.'

Mary grabbed a light and quietly opened the door. A shadowy figure hid in the darkness and Mary knew that someone needed her help.

'What is it? Is someone sick? Are they whipping one of the women?'

'No, Ma, it's babies. By the turn in the track before you arrive at Akim, they're beside the hollow tree.'

With that Mary grabbed a shawl and a bag and rushed out into the night. This time perhaps she would get there in time. Perhaps this time the babies wouldn't die, cold and hungry in the bush.

'How can they leave helpless children to die in the jungle? It's inhumane!'

Mary stopped. It couldn't be far now. She listened hard. 'What was that?' Mary gasped as in the distance a thin wail was heard. 'Was it a bird? An animal killing its prey? It might have been a baby?' Mary hurried on. She had to get there in time. She had to save them.

Peering through the darkness Mary searched for the hollow tree. There was nothing. Running on down the track she pushed her way through creepers and bush. Finally she found the clearing. There on the ground a large clay pot lay in the dirt.

Looking into the pot Mary realised she had arrived too late. Picking up the two dead baby girls, Mary sobbed her heart out.

Burying the two infants in the soft earth to the side of the clearing, Mary said a quick prayer. She prayed that next time she would be on time. Then she set off into the night.

Mary arrived at the mission station just as the first sunbeams pierced the outskirts of the forest. Tired and despondent, she slumped into a chair and slept. She was only woken by one of the African girls, anxiously whispering in her ear and shaking her shoulder.

'Ma! Ma! There is someone to see you. A white trader has come and he says he has something to show you.'

Mary rose from her chair, rubbing her stiff neck. She was in no mood to bargain with a white trader over western goods and trinkets. The only western product she allowed in the house was tea. A cup of tea would always be Mary's one weakness. But, grumbling slightly, she made her way down the steps to meet the rough bearded man. He held a bundle under his left arm. Mary wondered what it was. As she came closer she gasped. The trader removed the sacking to reveal the face of a very young baby girl.

Mary gasped! She was so glad that after the disappointment of the night before, here was a child who had survived.

'A baby girl,' Mary exclaimed. 'Where did you find her?' The man looked around. Mary suddenly realised the danger they were both in and ushered the unshaven, unkempt man into the hut. If any of the other village people should see them it might cause difficulties.

'I found her up river,' he sighed. 'She's only a day or two old. She was in a clay pot with her brother.'

'Oh, did he die?'

'No. I have him too, but I hid him in my canoe and must go back for him. Will you look after them?'

'Of course!'

'You'll have to be careful. If people start hearing that you're taking in twins they might turn against you.'

The man handed Mary the little girl, who whimpered slightly in her sleep. 'I managed to feed them some milk that I got from a tribeswoman a few miles further on. But I think I was watched. I'm sure someone was in the bush the night I picked the children up.'

Mary remembered her own experience as the trader continued to talk. 'If the family find out the children are here, they will stop at nothing to get at them.'

Mary then had a brainwave!

'I know what we will do. There is a Christian woman, three miles from here. I can trust her. She will look after the boy for a few weeks and then I will take him in too. That will mean that the villagers will just think they are two normal orphans. They won't be suspicious.'

Leaving the baby girl with an African helper, Mary followed the trader to his canoe. She cradled the baby boy in her arms as the trader waved goodbye.

'You are alive!' she whispered to the baby. 'You are alive! So many others haven't made it but you have! You and your darling little sister have been saved.'

Mary's friend gladly took the little boy in. Two weeks later the villagers saw Mary with another little orphan baby.

'It's a boy this time, Ma. He will be company for your little girl, won't he?'

Mary smiled. 'Yes. I have two babies now.'

***

The months that followed brought some sad news. Mrs Anderson and Mrs Sutherland were both dead. Other missionaries had also fallen ill and were in danger. Staff morale was low and the numbers were dwindling. Thankfully Mary had a few African girls living in with her, helping her with the mission work, the children and the schooling at times. This allowed Mary to go off on journeys into the bush, exploring new areas and meeting new tribesmen and women.

On one journey Mary met Okon, the tribal chief of a village called Ibaka. He had asked Mary to come and visit his village.

Before she left to visit him, many of the Old Town residents begged her to stay. 'It's too dangerous,' they pleaded. 'The weather is going to get very bad. If you are travelling and a squall hits, you will be in big trouble!'

'You will have to have trained boatmen to take you down the river at least!'

Mary smiled, 'That is not a problem. Chief Okon has agreed to send his own canoe for me. It's only a journey of thirty miles. Everything will be fine.'

But King Eyo's pride was hurt and he would only allow Mary to travel if she used his canoe. So Mary consented. However, when the brightly painted canoe finally arrived, it was late afternoon instead of the early morning that had been promised. Mary looked at the freshly painted decorations on the canoe and realised that King Eyo had made an effort to impress her, as well as Chief Okon. The whole village came out to see the goings on. The magnificent canoe ploughed through the river. The boatmen drove the paddles into the water and heaved them back out in time to a rhythmic chant. 'Ho, Ho, Ho.'

By the time all the arrangements had been made and goodbyes said it was getting late. Mary was mildly annoyed at the waste of time. But, with lit torches made out of dried reeds, they soon had enough light to see them on their way down the river. Then the chant changed to, 'Ho, Ho, Ho. Our beautiful Ma is with us.'

Mary waved goodbye to her friends and colleagues. The two babies were being nursed in the arms of a couple of the African helpers and Mary felt that she could leave everything with peace of mind. Now what would this visit to Chief Okon and the Ibaka tribe hold for her, she wondered?

Double Trouble

Mary wasn't certain what she would find at Ibaka. But the steady rhythm of the canoe, and the regular beating of the paddles against the water, soon lulled her to sleep. The next thing she heard was the sound of the paddles being drawn back inside the canoe to make ready for landing. Sitting bolt upright, she woke to the vibrant gold of the African sunrise flashing in streaks across the sky.

She was escorted from the canoe like a chief and King Eyo's men showed considerable pride in their 'Ma Akamba'. When she arrived at the Ibaka settlement, Mary was treated with great ceremony and even given Chief Okon's own hut to stay in.

Her presence, however, caused great curiosity among the women. The chief's wives sat at the door discussing every single thing that she did.

'Oh, look, it's true, she eats just like us. She puts food in her mouth and chews it and, yes, she swallows it in the same way that we do.'

Other young girls ran up to Mary, giggling, touched her skin then ran away again, laughing. It was all so new and exciting for them to see a white woman. But the most awkward situation for Mary was the sleeping arrangements. The chief gave her the great honour of having her sleep beside all his wives, who were very large women. Every one of them insisted on sleeping as close to Mary as she could which meant that during the night Mary would wake almost smothered by large bodies. Each woman was tall, strong and very insistent on honouring Mary with her presence.

Mary's duties throughout the next few days were mostly medical. She treated boils and sores, disinfected and cleaned cuts, bandaged wounds and burns. Then she held services. She wanted to leave them with a little of the God she loved, a flavour of his goodness. But the audiences did not understand. Mary found it very tiring.

A few days before she was due to return, Mary noticed that the Chief Okon's wives were not as chatty as usual. They had very anxious faces. Mary knew that something was up.

'What's happened?' she asked.

'Two young wives have done a very bad thing,' explained one of the older wives. 'They were caught last night leaving their compound and going to the house of a young man.'

Mary knew that no proper investigation would be made into whether the girls were innocent or guilty. Mary also knew that the punishment was 100 lashes.

'They won't survive,' she gasped, and ran straight to the palaver house to investigate. Mary pleaded with Chief Okon to let her speak on the girls' behalf. Reluctantly he agreed and let her enter the palaver house to represent the young women.

Straightaway Mary went up to the girls and lectured them about their wicked behaviour. Mary knew that if she didn't do this immediately the tribal elders would throw her out of the palaver house before she could do anything. To gain the trust of the men she had to chastise the women first. The men agreed with Mary's strict lecture and felt that Ma Akamba was really on their side. Then Mary turned on them 'Your behaviour's a disgrace.' They looked at her shocked. 'Cooping up young girls. Giving them to old men who already have more wives than they know what to do with. These girls have a right to expect more out of life than being penned up in a yard with a bunch of other women. This is all your fault!'

The men got up and started shouting at Mary, shaking their fists and yelling. They said that they had asked her to come with 'God' but that they didn't want 'God' any more. Mary however, stood her ground and at the end of the palaver she had reduced the girls' sentence to ten lashes each.

After the punishment the girls ran into her hut and lay quivering on the floor, blood streaming out of the cuts on their backs, sobbing and screaming with the pain. Mary bandaged their backs well to stop flies getting at them. For the rest of her stay they lay on the floor of Mary's hut, whimpering in shock and barely conscious.

Days later Mary had to leave them, uncertain what might happen to the girls. They could be banished from the village, disgraced, left to fend for themselves, or it could all be forgotten as it so often was in Africa.

This time Mary bundled up her belongings into a smaller canoe belonging to Okon and set off for home.

After a horrific storm and a near sinking, Mary arrived at Old Town with a raging fever. The fever kept her in bed for over a week. Then there was the bad news. Not everything had gone smoothly at Old Town while she was away. The African helpers had not been able to protect the twins. It seemed as though the white trader had been right and he had been watched. Though how the family found out where the twins were being kept was beyond Mary's understanding.

She couldn't believe that they had found the children so quickly, kidnapped the little boy and left without a trace. Mary knew that the little boy was now dead. She was just thankful that the little girl was all right.

Mary's fever still raged. The tornado that had struck the village had done no good for her health. The mission brought her back to Duke Town. Mary arrived there, to the surprise of everyone, nursing a little girl. 'I've still got you, little one. And I shall call you Janie, just like my little sister at home. You are now my baby, my special baby.'

There was no arguing with her. Mary and the little girl were together. Where Mary went Janie went and that meant Scotland. The monthly steamer had arrived at Duke Town and, for once, a quick decision was made. Mary and the baby were placed on the steamer. The fear was that Mary was dying so she had to go home now. Perhaps she wouldn't even make the voyage home? She did look really ill this time.

However, when Mary and Janie arrived in Scotland her mother and sisters were there to help. And remarkably Mary had undergone a strong recovery on board the boat.

Over the months that followed, Mary's strength improved and her speaking engagements increased. The Mission Board realised that, as well as having a bright and enthusiastic missionary on leave, there was also an excellent visual aid accompanying her.

The baby was an instant attraction. Here was the reason for the whole mission. This little baby and thousands like her was what it was all about. The money just poured in and when Mary announced her intention to return to Calabar the Board asked her to postpone things for a while. They needed more recruits and finance. Mary's speaking tours were bringing in donations and more interest than ever before. They just couldn't afford to let her go.

Eventually Mary was asked to return but not to Old Town. She was needed in Creek Town as the missionaries there were too ill to continue. Mary agreed reluctantly.

Just before she was due to depart, however, disaster struck. Mary's sister, Janie, fell ill with tuberculosis. Frantic plans were made to move her and Mrs Slessor to a warmer climate, and eventually a house was found for them in Devon, England. Susan remained in Dundee and Mary travelled down to Devon to settle her mother and sister into the new home. However, after just a few weeks in Devon, Mary received tragic news from Dundee. Susan had suddenly fallen ill and died.

Mary had to return to Dundee to bury Susan and close up the house. 'How can I leave Ma and Janie now? I can't leave them alone like this.' Mary didn't know what she should do. Mrs Slessor then fell ill and, just when Mary couldn't postpone her return to Calabar any longer, a friend volunteered to look after the two invalids.

Mary, thirty-seven years old, returned to Calabar. But she anxiously awaited the first steamer to arrive with the post.

The first letter she received said that both her mother and sister were well. However, three months later Mary received news that both her mother and her sister, Janie, had died. Mary's heart broke. But as she dried her tears and the following weeks drew her further into her work, she realised that her last ties with Scotland had been severed.

'Heaven is now nearer to me than Britain,' she wrote, 'and there will be no one anxious for me now if I go up country.' Mary immediately put in a formal application to the Mission Board to go to the Okoyong tribe.

Boiling Oil

'What does she think she is doing? Is she mad?'
The conversation buzzed round the mission. Mary
knew what they were saying. She knew that they had
grounds to be worried for her. The Okoyong tribe
were the fearless head-hunters, the arch enemy of
the Efik tribes. They had banned all missionaries
from their land. Perhaps she was mad? But she was
mad for God.

Mary eventually got things going. An initial visit
to the Okoyong went favourably and they agreed
to give her ground to build a hut on. This ground
would be sacred, and all who needed refuge could
use Mary's ground as a bolt hole. No weapons would
ever enter her compound. She and all within her
walls would be completely safe.

On the 4th of August 1888 Mary made her
journey into the unknown – the first of many. She
took with her little Janie and quite a few other
children who were now part of Mary's African family.
When Mary arrived at Ekenge she discovered that
the two villages of Ifako and Ekenge were celebrating

a funeral. Mary knew this could be a dangerous situation. Someone of importance at Ifako had died, and the inhabitants were celebrating in the usual orgy of drinking and killing. Gun shots reverberated around the forests, screams and death shrieks filled the air. Every adult within a ten mile radius was an immediate threat to both her and her children.

The children were shivering and crying, clearly terrified. Mary, hands on hips, started to look around anxiously for the promised supplies which should have been following her. 'The crew men are supposed to be here by now. What can have happened to them?'

Mary was in a dilemma. She couldn't leave the children alone – it was too dangerous – but she needed supplies. They needed food, medicine, clothing and other provisions.

Just then an official in charge of the expedition burst through the forest, covered in mud and flustered. 'They won't come, Miss Slessor, I am here to tell you that there is nothing that will persuade the crew to leave the boat. They say they are too tired.'

Mary simmered gently, her temper bubbling away under the surface of her weather-beaten skin. 'Too tired!' she suddenly burst out. 'Too tired! Just wait!' Mary knew that this was one big excuse.

Leaving the children with the official, Mary made her way to the launch. The sleepy boatmen were snoring, soundly. All snugly tucked up under the tarpaulin.

'Get up! Get up!' Mary shouted. With her umbrella she hammered on top of the tarpaulin until all the sleepers were up and rubbing their heads, confused and slightly annoyed. Mary bullied and cajoled them into taking her provisions to the village.

Mary forged ahead of them, swinging her battered old umbrella.

As she made the journey for the third time that night, tired and hungry, she thought about what lay ahead for her and for her children. Little Janie, just learning to toddle, and the other children, were now in a dangerous situation. But Mary couldn't have left them behind. They were hers and she loved them dearly. This gentle side to Mary was seldom seen by anybody these days, except the children. Mary was rough and she was tough, but she was also loving and gentle and she chose carefully who saw the gentle side. She knew that for the African chiefs to be a little bit afraid of her was a protection.

She was roughest with those she saw as most deserving of it. The native aristocracy had scant regard for the lives of slaves or women and Mary couldn't stomach that. But she longed for these people to learn of her Jesus. Mary's skill with people was a great asset as she chose day by day, hour by hour, how best to behave with the people she met. Did this man need bullying or should she cajole him a little? Would the chief stop the flogging if she screamed at him or if she flattered him? She almost always got it right.

But as they drew near the village of Ekenge, Mary knew that before she could tackle the bloody customs of this particular tribe, she would have to establish a relationship with them.

'I can't just go in here and expect them all to jump to my tune immediately. These people have no idea who Jesus Christ is, they have no idea who I am and I'm just here for as long as they will allow me to stay. I have to get to know them first. I pray that eventually they will come to love and respect me, and then come to love and respect my God.

Mary never forced the Bible down a tribe's throats. However, she didn't avoid teaching and preaching either. It was her aim, as soon as possible, to set up services, to teach God's truth and to leave God to open up the hearts.

The first expedition to this area had gone quite well in Mary's estimation. She had met Chief Edem and his sister, Eme, who had become an instant friend. That was a friendship that would last for life. 'I'm sure that she will become a Christian one day,' thought

Mary. 'I wouldn't be surprised if she was amongst the first converts.'

Mary remembered the church service she had held on that first visit. It had been a sunnier, more pleasant day, and there hadn't been any murders or drinking going on. So when Mary held her service, the whole atmosphere had been pleasant and friendly as the Okoyong gathered round, curious to see and hear the goings on.

Snapping out of her daydream, Mary shivered again as she heard the awful sounds. She caught glimpses of fires and leaping figures in the dark. She hurried the boat men on. They needed little encouragement. Mary prayed silently to the Lord God. 'Father, I myself cannot do anything with a people like this, no one could. I will just leave them to you.'

As the packages and bundles were unpacked at the hut the children huddled round her for some security. Mary sighed as she kissed the little chubby Janie on the forehead. Deftly she slung the little child over her back in the same way that the native women carried their little children. Then she set to work.

It was several days before the people of Ekenge began to trickle back to their homes. Mary put two and two together and decided that everyone who was still alive would probably be nursing huge hangovers. Angrily she brushed some of the dust off her dress and glared at the silent huts. Some days later Edem visited Mary and insisted that she live in his compound. Mary didn't relish this idea. It might mean less freedom. But when Edem assured her that her hut would still be a place of refuge she agreed. Mary decided that she would wait a while before asking for a new compound of her own.

Mary worked hard in the next few months to set up the basic services for the people. Medicines were prescribed and, as usual, the white man's medicine was a great pull. News of its power spread by word of mouth, and soon many people were coming for pills and treatment. But Mary soon found out that some men were putting the pills in their mouths and not swallowing them. They wanted to keep the pills as lucky charms to hang around their necks! To tackle this problem Mary would promptly punch the men in the stomach. Shocked, the men had no option but to swallow the pill immediately.

Mary did find the atmosphere in the villages trying. Alcohol was drunk daily by the men and the women. 'Everybody drinks here,' she wrote in her journal. 'I lie down at night knowing that not a sober man or woman lies within several miles of my hut. The hut too deserves a mention as I am living in a single apartment with a mud floor, surrounded on every side by men, women, children, goats, dogs, fowls, cats and even rats.'

Mary put the pen down and sighed. 'It's a bit crowded.'

***

Many months had passed when Mary sat back and took a look at what she had accomplished, with God's help, since her arrival. There weren't any converts and teaching Christianity was still an uphill struggle but she was encouraged. 'I think they're accepting me now. They trust me.' The Okoyong were beginning to look on Mary as their friend.

Mary's acceptance was put to the test one day when a terrified man ran into her hut.

'Ma, you must come, quick. The chief's wife has much pain. Come quick.'

Quickly she grabbed her medicine chest. Following, at quite a pace, she soon arrived at the compound of a local chief and was ushered in to see a young woman lying on a bed groaning. Mary knew that this was an important patient, and that if she failed to cure her some would try to blame her for the death.

After some questions to Chief Edem, Mary discovered the problem. Edem had in fact bitten his wife in a drunken rage and the bite was now infected. Mary breathed a sigh of relief. It was a simple diagnosis and cure. In a matter of days the young woman was fit and well and Mary's fame spread. Edem was very grateful and the rest of the chiefs very impressed. Mary had cured one of the Okoyong aristocracy. Mary's reputation was secure.

Over the years she continued to add to the legend of Ma Akamba. One day an important Ekenge chief purchased a beautiful slave girl. The girl did not want to be attached to this old man. She was in love with another. One night she escaped to his hut to ask him to run away with her. The male slave refused the girl. She went into the forest and killed herself.

However, she had been seen going to the male slave's hut and, as a result, he was accused of bewitching the young woman. The palaver house discussed his case quickly and sentenced him to flogging and execution. Mary, who attended the trial, jumped to her feet. She protested that this whole trial was absolutely unjust. 'There is no evidence that he did anything to the girl.'

The chiefs looked at her shocked and enraged. Here was a woman, and a white woman at that, daring to question their methods of justice. But Mary carried on. This made the chiefs and officials even more angry. Everybody began to shout and some of the chiefs came right up to Mary and yelled in her face, waving fists and sticks at her. However, Mary stood her ground. She knew that she could not show any fear, for that would be fatal.

'If I give up now they will lose all respect for me.'

Slowly but surely the chiefs calmed down and agreed to rethink the situation. Perhaps a compromise could be reached. The chiefs agreed to a flogging but no execution. Mary bowed her head and thanked the chiefs for their justice.

That night she heard the screams of the tortured man through the walls of her hut. It was a torture to listen to it too but Mary was thankful that the man would survive. There would be no execution.

In the future Mary Slessor would often make her views known in local justice and politics. Soon she would not only tackle day to day tribal customs but also religious ones. For now she watched her step.

But she never got used to the frantic, terrifying, sounds she heard at night. They still chilled her to the bone.

'If I did not know that my Saviour is near me I would go out of my mind,' Mary wrote one evening.

***

A few months after her arrival, Mary decided to set up an official school to teach alphabet and sums to the local children as well as the adults. Free men and slaves, as well as women, attended the classes. She taught them the Efik language and alphabet as that would be the one most useful to them in trading with the outside world.

'If they learn to speak this language they will soon learn about how tribes like the Efik live, with money for food, medicines and other provisions, they will want this too. They will see the buildings that are being built in places like Duke Town and will have ideas of their own. If they start spending their time building and trading they will have far less time for getting drunk.'

Mary's plans were sensible and her schemes for the economic and spiritual growth of the area were remarkable.

She was still the fierce, bristling, redhead however. The Okoyong never doubted the strength of her temper. One evening trouble was brewing yet again in the Ekenge village.

'This woman was caught in adultery!' was the accusation, as a young wife was dragged up before the tribal officials. The story ran like this:

A slave had been doing work for a man in the village. This man had a wife who was at home when her husband was called away on business. Alone with the slave, the woman stayed in the house while the slave worked outside. Then the slave asked the woman for some food. She refused, as giving food to a man who is not your husband is the same as a promise to commit adultery with him. The slave accused her of starving him. To keep the peace she agreed to give the slave a small piece of yam which was to keep him going until her husband returned home.

However, someone saw her give the yam, and accusations flowed. The chiefs tried to keep the trial a secret from Mary. She only knew that something was happening when the drums began to ring out. As Mary ran to the palaver house she heard the woman's screams. The Egbo officials were tying her up with cords. She was spread-eagled on the ground and screaming. She was to be covered in boiling oil. Her naked body was writhing in an attempt to get away from the steaming pot.

The chiefs sat watching the proceedings. The whole village was drunk on gin and blood. And into the middle marched Mary, who placed herself in between the fire and the girl. The village plunged into silence.

The masked official advanced on Mary with the ladle swinging. High and wide it waved as he danced, leering and drooling around her. Mary remained between him and the girl. This time it wasn't a lead weight being swung inches from her face, it was a ladle full of burning oil. She couldn't negotiate, but she could still stand her ground and stare at him, eyeball to eyeball.

The drunken bully chickened out under Mary's steely gaze, and the officials gathered round to discuss what was to be done. Mary asked Edem to release the girl. Edem looked at this fiery, scary woman and gave in immediately.

Edem allowed Mary to take the girl to her hut for safety. In a few days, in typical African fashion, the situation was forgotten about. The girl held Mary's hand as she stepped outside the compound for the first time since the trial. Dark brown eyes looked deep into silver blue eyes and they both smiled. The young wife silently slipped through the forest, back to her home and the arms of her young husband.

Mary breathed a sigh of relief. 'Thank you, Lord, for giving that girl the gift of life, but you have another gift to give these people. You want to give them yourself, and that's the best gift they could ever have. But how do I start, God? How do I start?'

Mary Meets her Match

Mary decided that she should start as she meant to go on, and begin proper services in Ekenge and Ifako. Now was the time to make services part of the local culture. Mary preached in the evenings once a week at both Ifako and Ekenge. She struggled on, undeterred by the village chaos as children and chickens competed with teaching and singing.

Often Mary had to battle with something more serious – confusion. She would look out at the puzzled congregation and realise that she wasn't getting through to them. The people found it so difficult to think about a loving and caring God who wasn't vindictive. Their gods were unreliable, except in their thirst for blood and sacrifices. Mary's God cared for them. They found that hard to swallow. This God said that all were equal in his sight. He loved both rich and poor, slave and free. To the Okoyong, this was earth-shattering. Did this God really think that slaves held just as much worth as free people? Was a woman just as important as a man? Did this God really say that men should love their wives?

Mary realised that this might take a long time to sink in, and that it was good she had started now and not later.

There was a part of the service that the Okoyong people loved greatly, and that was singing. Mary's experience had taught her the value of a good sing-song. The Okoyong loved to join in with Mary's hymns. She translated some really rousing English words into really rousing Efik.

Many evening services went on and on into the night. The moon would light up the flickering fireflies as they danced in the clearings. The voices of the villagers accompanied this dance as the evening fires died down.

As the months and years passed, villagers began to trust Mary and her God. Her one regret was that Edem and Eme never totally turned from the old ways. Eme would worship Mary's God when Mary was there and her own gods at other times. Edem never believed in Christ, even when many from his tribe believed. They loved Mary and trusted her, but they never trusted Mary's God, even though they did all in their power to help their new friend. For instance, there was a day that Mary finally met her match and that match was Eme.

It happened on a night when the tribe's warrior women invaded the village. They were a band of female warriors who had all been born in the same year. They did not merely drag away the bodies from a battle, but actively took part in the killing. However, at that point in time there was no fighting to be done so the women had to make their living in other ways. This meant robbing and invading the villages. This particular band of women had heard of the white woman at Ekenge. They charged into the village, firing their guns and shouting, waving swords and torches in the air. They looked a dreadful sight with their naked bodies painted in ghoulish chalk designs. The warriors demanded to see Mary and insisted that she should give them money and other gifts.

However, Chief Edem was having none of it. Mary was Ekenge's missionary and she must not be harmed. Mary was having none of it either. She was all for going out there and giving these women a piece of her mind. But Edem and Eme knew that the threats of the warriors were not false ones. When Mary made for the door, Eme got in front, her huge stature blocking the doorway. Mary made to push past her, but Eme stood her ground, just as stubborn as Mary. With one hand she gently pushed the bristling redhead back into the hut. 'Ma, you will stay,' was all the large woman said, and Mary meekly sat back down on the floor.

Edem went out once again to negotiate with the band of women warriors, and soothed their anger with the promise of a generous gift of rum. Soon the women left to cause trouble elsewhere.

Mary was suddenly struck by the danger she had been in. Edem remained stone-cold sober as he stood guard with his men at the door of Mary's hut that night. Mary realised that these warrior women must have been more lethal than she had at first realised. She was thankful for Eme's strength of will and body. 'No one else would have managed to keep me in the hut,' she muttered to herself.

Finally Edem decided that Mary's hut, even though it was in his own compound, was not suitable for the town missionary. 'We will build our Ma Akamba a house for herself.' Mary smiled, now sure that the Okoyong had accepted her as one of their own.

Romance at Last?

Mary realised that one evening of abstinence didn't mean a teetotal tribe. As Mary and her children settled into their new house, Mary revisited the commerce idea as a way to get the Okoyong off drink and on to more fruitful pastimes. Often she would argue with Eme and Edem and the other chiefs about the stupidity of drink.

'Don't you see how fuddled you are when you've been drinking? You were sober that night you thought I might be attacked in my hut. Why was that?'

Edem would look up at the sky or down at his feet; he didn't like it when Mary began to get annoyed with him. 'You knew,' she continued 'that you and your men would not be at your best if you were drunk. You knew that these women would have come back and carried me off, and you would have been too drunk to do anything!'

Mary sighed; for it was so frustrating to see the tribe waste their money on imported alcohol and waste their abilities by drinking it. 'I have made some progress with the women,' she would admit to herself, 'and there was that young chief who came to me the other day boasting that he had stayed off drink for three whole days.' Mary laughed. It sounded so ludicrous. Three whole days was no great success in Mary's mind. She had seen her father in his time turn off drink for weeks, only to go back to it at the first temptation.

'But first steps first,' decided Mary. The tribe had at least agreed to their first trip to trade with the Efik tribe. That in itself was a major step forward. It had only been three or four years since Mary had first arrived here, and the Okoyong had then been the Efik's committed enemies. It was a landmark victory for Mary. And she sincerely hoped that it was a sign of better things to come.

After much cajoling, bullying and pestering, the Okoyong finally set off with Mary to visit King Eyo. The expedition involved a couple of false starts as the Okoyong overloaded their canoe and the whole thing capsized in the river. Mary had an awful time persuading them that this was not a bad omen, just stupidity on their part. Eventually she got them to rescue their produce and reload it in a bigger canoe.

When they arrived at Creek Town, where King Eyo resided, Mary was pleased at how the day went. Eyo was the picture of respectability and was courteous and friendly to his old enemies. He too realised that if this day went well it could herald great things for the Okoyong and Efik tribes. As Eyo inspected the fruits and farm produce, he had only praise for the high quality. He was generous when it came to the final price negotiations, and the Okoyong tribesmen returned home, heroes, to their wives and families.

Mary returned home to her ever-growing family. Janie, now seven years old, was a good little organiser, and was taking on more of the responsibilities with the younger children. 'The day went really well,' Mary told her daughter. 'They even had discussions about tribal relations which was more than I had hoped for. King Eyo has agreed to send his traders to the Ekenge landing place to pick up their goods in future, and he has even agreed to lend the Okoyong canoes.'

'That's great news,' exclaimed Janie. 'Nobody round here has a decent canoe.'

'That's right,' laughed Mary, as she remembered the chaos earlier on. 'But they'll soon sort that. The men are already planning their own fleet of canoes.'

'Your plan is working then, Ma!', laughed Janie.

'Yes, the more time they spend using their hands the less time they will have for drinking themselves stupid. The other thing is that Chief Edem has seen the wonderful houses in Creek Town. He wants our one to look just as good. Though how on earth we are going to get windows and stairs built into this house without a carpenter is anybody's guess.'

'We'll wait and see,' said Janie wisely, and Mary nodded.

Mary's first report from Ekenge was printed in the Missionary Record of March 1889. And a carpenter called Mr Ovens just happened to be reading the paper while on holiday in Edinburgh from America. He was so convicted by Mary's courage in such difficult circumstances that he did an incredible thing. He immediately changed his return ticket to America for an outgoing ticket to Calabar. Accepted by the Foreign Mission Board, Mr Ovens, the carpenter, made his way out to help Miss Slessor put in her windows and her stairs.

Meanwhile, Mary fell ill again. She had been under an immense strain for months. In the end, she was forced to return to Duke Town with her family.

'Just when we were making progress too, Janie. How discouraging.'

Janie took Mary's hand and held it, wiping her fevered brow and easing her into a more comfortable position. 'What would I do without you, my Janie, my wonderful Janie?'

Janie smiled, 'What would I have done without you, my wonderful Ma?'

As they arrived at Duke Town, Mary might have been forgiven for thinking that this would again be another stressful, tedious visit to the stiffly-starched mission house. She felt more at home in the bush than in the polite society of Duke Town. But then this time something was different. Mary met someone special. His name was Charles Morrison, a teacher and scholar, who had joined the mission to take over the training of the African teachers. Mary was almost twice his age. He was in his early twenties, she was in her early forties by this time. She was the older missionary, recovering from an illness. He was the new recruit, sympathetic and bookish, eager to discuss what he had read with the sick missionary. And Mary, who still avidly read and re-read all she got her hands on, relished the discussion and mental stimulation.

'You will write to me,' the anxious young man enquired, as Mary prepared to return to her tribe.

'Yes, Charlie, I will write, gladly,' and Mary smiled warmly at this gentle and engaging young man. But it would be some time before Mary would meet Charles again. Meanwhile Mr Ovens was busy hammering at her house, knocking up a staircase and sawing out space in the walls for windows. It was a big operation. Every morning, except Sunday, Ovens would be out in the yard with his wide-brimmed hat, calculating some angle that he needed to be sure of before building the staircase. Mary would smile, secretly to herself, as she noticed the stir that this new visitor was causing. The Okoyong had never built a two-storey house before, and they watched Mr Ovens very closely to see how it was done. The young men did as Mary had always hoped they would, and started to build their own buildings with stairs. Chief Edem even sent to Creek Town for glass to put in his house as windows. The drinking problem didn't disappear overnight, but it did get less frequent.

Then, just as Mary had felt that things were going so well, disaster struck. Mr Ovens dashed into the house, 'Mary, quick. It's Edem's son, Etim. He's been hurt.'

Mary again grabbed her medicine chest and ran along the bush path with Mr Ovens. 'What happened?' she gasped, as they turned a corner on the trail.

'He was cutting down a branch from a tree. He's been renovating his house over the last few weeks. The branch fell on top of him and he is unconscious.' As they came across the group of anxious friends and relatives in the clearing where Etim had been working, Mary felt sick to the stomach. This was serious and she had suspicions that it was beyond her skill to do anything for the young man. Mr Ovens looked at Mary, anxiously. 'I know it's bad Mary, but why are you looking so awful?'

Mary then explained the situation. 'Etim is a chief's son. If he dies there will be a big funeral. That will mean a lot of drinking and ritual killings. If Etim doesn't recover there is going to be a blood-bath.'

Mr Oven's face paled as he realised the implications of the accident. Mary's mind was working overtime. She ordered a stretcher to be made for the young man, and that he be brought to her house straight away. She would do her best for him, and meanwhile she would try to think one step ahead of everyone else. She must be ready for the worst.

'If he dies there is bound to be the usual accusation of all the old enemies. There will be a poison bean trial or strangling or something. This could put us back years,' grimaced Mary, as she tenderly bathed Etim's forehead and tried to make sure he took some water by dripping it through his lips and gently rubbing his throat. Mary waited. Over the next few weeks Etim's life hung in the balance. The people were distraught and his father was worst. Mary sighed as she looked again at the unconscious Etim.

'Shall I go for the doctor?' asked Ovens. Mary shook her head. 'There's no point now. I've known for some time that Etim isn't going to make it. His injuries are too serious. No, Mr Ovens, we are just going to have to sit this one out and try and think ahead.'

Mary came into her house one day to find Chief Edem and the witch doctor shouting at Etim. The witch doctor then blew smoke and potions into Etim's ears, and all his wives started screaming and wailing. Running outside Mary hit her fists against the wall. The people were trying to cast out evil spirits.

'Has nothing that I have told them sunk in at all?' Mary wondered.

Then Mary heard the proclamation of the witch doctor which chilled her to the bone. 'What did he say?' asked Ovens, who had come down from doing something on the roof.

'He's just blamed one of the other villages. If we don't do something there will be a blood bath tonight, and that's even before Etim has died.'

Mary stamped her foot and glared at the witch doctor who was now disappearing along the track with Edem and some of the other officials following after.

Someone came out and told Mary that, during the witch doctor's ceremonies, Etim had died. Mary groaned, prayed, and then acted as the men of the village rushed off to get prisoners. Mary had precious little time to lose.

'What I am going to do now may seem quite strange and you and others will probably strongly disagree with me, but you have to understand we are trying to stop a blood-bath.' Ovens listened intently. 'I am going to lay out Etim's body in a very grand style. It is very important to the Okoyong that a chief's son is well laid out, with provisions and clothes and things for his journey into the other world.' Ovens looked a bit doubtful. Mary pleaded. 'I know it's heathen, I know that it goes against everything that we believe in, but you've never seen one of these funerals before. We have to stop it somehow!'

Mary then went back into the house and took a shirt, suit and tie from a missionary barrel, as well as some silk material to tie round Etim's waist. She placed coloured feathers and a top hat on his head. Then, carefully, Edem's wives placed him under a large striped umbrella in the courtyard for all to see. Mary even put a mirror in front of the corpse. This really impressed the Okoyong people. As they walked past, they noted how Etim was the first Chief's son to have a mirror laid in front of him. They thought that he would be very pleased to see himself looking so distinguished.

Mary didn't know if she was relieved or sickened by the whole situation. Then she had another idea. 'One of the old missionaries was in a situation like this in the early days of the Calabar mission. He defused an explosive situation after a funeral with a magic lantern show. There's one at Duke Town. We should send for it.'

'I'll send my assistant to get it,' agreed Ovens.

The magic lantern show was like a slide show today. Pictures could be shown on it. Mary knew there was one at the mission house with pictures of horses and carriages and other western wonders.

'It may get their minds off killing and murdering,' Mary hoped.

Still Mary continued to work. 'We must make a very grand coffin,' she said to Ovens. 'These people must feel that this funeral is unique and spectacular. Perhaps they will feel that there is no need for Etim to have slaves or women killed. See, they already have some people tied up in the yard.'

Ovens looked at where Mary was pointing and gasped. Three women with babies in their arms were tied up in the burning midday heat. Other slaves were being fastened to stakes. Then Mary noticed the witch doctor cradling something in his hand. Others were gathered round egging him on.

'Oh no!' Mary cried. 'It's a poison bean trial. They're going to poison the prisoners. They believe that when people die from the trial it means they are guilty; if they survive they are innocent. That never happens, by the way, they're eating poison after all.'

Mary ran over to start negotiating with Chief Edem, who was overseeing the trial.

All of Mary's skill with tribal tradition and custom was called on when negotiating for the lives of the women and the slaves. For several days and nights Mary haggled and cajoled until twenty-one days after Etim's death, all the slaves were free. Then after the magic lantern show there was more talk about the horses and the buildings than about killing and revenge.

After everything had calmed down, Mary was exhausted. Her four-year stint had been passed long ago, but there was no replacement ready. She refused to leave her tribe at such a critical moment. Eventually a volunteer was found who would run the mission at Ekenge and Ifako for one year and excitedly Mary wrote to Charles Morrison at Duke Town to tell him of her arrival. 'I will be in Duke Town for a few weeks before I leave for Scotland. We will be able to resume our old discussions about books and things. I am looking forward to seeing you again, my friend.' Charles was looking forward to it too, but for another reason. He had purchased a ring and intended that Mary should wear it as his fiancée.

The romance was a whirlwind, though they had been writing for a while. Mary and Charles didn't think about the age difference and, before she had left for Scotland with her children, Mary had accepted Charles' proposal of marriage, under one condition. 'You will have to come to Ekenge. I will never leave my work there.'

Charles agreed, and contacted the mission about his transfer from Duke Town to Ekenge.

When Mary arrived in Scotland, after a brief winter in Devon, she went to a photographer's to have a picture taken of her wearing Charles' ring. At that point the engagement was secret and Mary had yet to approach the Mission Board with her intentions for marriage.

When she did, the Board were surprised to say the least. '

Some humming and hawing took place and then a decision.

'His job is too important, Miss Slessor. We can't allow him to leave Duke Town until we have a replacement.'

Perhaps they realised that Charles was a physically weak young man? Perhaps they thought that this was just an example of a middle-aged female missionary desperate for a little love and affection? However, what with her family history and her parents' volatile relationship, marriage was certainly something Mary would not have entered into lightly.

But it just wasn't to be. Back at Duke Town, Charles fell ill and the engagement was quietly broken off.

When she was back with her Okoyong tribe, Mary heard that Charles was now travelling back to his family in America. The final chapter in this sad romance was when Mary heard that Charles' house and manuscripts, all his life's work, had been burnt to a crisp in a fire. Soon after this tragedy Charles himself died, and Mary turned back to her original plan of singleness. Putting Charles to the back of her mind, she refocused on the work in hand.

However, for the rest of her life Mary had three books that always went with her, the well-worn Bible with the writing crammed into the margins and two other books. Why she kept the two other books wasn't certain, but there were two signatures on their front pages, and these two signatures were side by side. Charles Morrison and Mary Slessor. That was all that remained of a very brief romance.

Back on Track

Janie's face broke into a grin as she looked at Mary perched on a three-legged stool nursing another couple of twins. 'Two boys this time, isn't it, Ma?'

'Yes Janie, and they're a pair, I can tell you. You can never feed them enough, they're aye hungry.' Mary looked long and deep into the beautiful brown eyes of the babies. They were just as she had pictured they would be so many years ago in cold Dundee. Mary remembered the dream of the little African child running out to her, crying, asking to be held, protected, loved. And here she was holding and protecting another little boy and his brother. 'How many children do you think we've looked after this year, Janie?'

'Don't ask me, Ma! Do we know how many children we have in the house at the moment?'

Mary thought a little and then said, 'Seventeen including these two here.'

Janie laughed, 'Here you are nearing fifty, with seventeen children running around your feet.'

Mary joined in the laughter. She remembered the

old children's rhyme about the old woman who lived in a shoe, she had so many children, she didn't know what to do. But Mary knew exactly what she was doing. For the first time in ages she felt that she was back to her old self. The other day she had sorted out another local squabble between some tribal chiefs.

What really convinced her that she was totally recovered was the adventure she had had the previous week. Gazing down at the little boys in her arms, Mary smiled, 'And it was all your fault, you poor little mites.'

Mary had heard that a woman in Ekenge had given birth to twins. She had tried time and time again to persuade the family to let her take them away to Duke Town. At least there she would know they were safe and out of harm's way. But there was disagreement amongst the family members. The final decision was that Mary should not take the children, and that they would deal with the twins in their own way.

Mary had tried everything. She had chastised them, joked with them, pleaded with them. Mary's skill with the local tongue was amazing. She used their phrases brilliantly, she even had their gestures and intonations down to a fine art. It was hard to tell the difference between someone born and bred in the Okoyong tribe and Mary Slessor, who had been born and bred in Scotland.

But as the night drew to a close Mary knew that none of her skills or persuasive powers would work. 'I have no time to dilly-dally here,' she said, annoyed. So Mary waited until everything was quiet, and snuck out of her house.

Quickly she flitted through the shadows, through some of the bush and scrub and over to the back of the house where the twins had been born. There was no sound. 'Are the twins still there?' Mary thought anxiously. Then she heard a whimper to her left and she breathed easy. 'They're still here.'

Carefully and quietly Mary started to peel back some of the rushes with which the native hut had been built. Quietly she made a hole in the wall that was big enough to reach through and grab the twins.

Finally, Mary shoved her head through the hole. The twins were within reach so she reversed out and shoved her arm in, grabbing one twin and then another. The babies started to scream and holler and Mary ran for it. Angry shouts and yells sounded out behind her as Mary's skinny legs beat a retreat through the bush. Panting, she arrived at the house, and Janie was there to meet her.

'You've got them, I see,' she said. And then looking up she added, 'And that will be the family charging down the road.'

Mary ran inside the house and slammed the door. 'First things first,' she gasped. 'I am going to get you two fed. It will probably be the first decent meal you will have had all week. Poor pets.'

Janie, meanwhile, was standing her ground outside the house explaining that Ma was not going to come outside and she most certainly was not going to give back the twins. An angry father and uncle stormed back to their compound. A nervous looking woman hung around outside Mary's hut before running after them.

'The mother?' asked Janie.

Mary nodded as she handed one of the children to Janie, along with a bottle. 'It's good that she hasn't been banished. Perhaps things are changing. But one thing is for certain, neither of these babies would have been safe in that house. The superstition is still too strong.' Mary sighed.

Mary wondered if the mother approved of what she had done. 'Is she glad her children have made it out alive?'

That night, however, a messenger came from Edem and Eme. Edem refused to come and visit Mary as long as the twins were in her house. She must come and visit him. The next day Mary sent Edem a letter saying, 'I am in my house just the same as ever I was.' She wasn't going to give in on this issue.

Over the next few weeks, though, things escalated. The villagers refused to come anywhere near Mary and so all medical treatment and schooling were stopped. However, Mary was worried about something else more serious.

Mary urgently called Janie.'

'One of the twins is really sick. I've tried everything. This morning he wouldn't drink and he was running a slight fever, but now the heat on his forehead is far worse. I think he is going to die!'

Janie gasped. After all their hard work, after the risks of running through the night and invading the home, snatching the babies and keeping them in the hut... the baby was going to die.

That night the baby did die and Mary wept. The following morning the baby was buried and the villagers started to come back. Mary sighed at their superstition. Edem and Eme came to her, smiling and relieved to be able to visit their missionary once again. Mary was glad to see them, but saddened too that they wouldn't come to see her as long as the twins had remained with her. They thought that the twin that had died must have been the devil twin and that the other living baby was all right.

Mary argued with them, but it accomplished nothing. Then, one day in 1895, when Mary was forty-seven years old, she had a very encouraging report to give the Foreign Mission Committee. 'The raiding, plundering and stealing of slaves has almost ceased. The killings at funerals is now a thing of the past, and it is a rare thing to see a woman drunk. Twins are still a problem, but I am usually given them before any harm is done. Women who come to my yard have been known to sit beside twins, and some have even touched them.'

Amongst the natives of Calabar Mary was now respected and trusted and some trusted her God, though not enough in Mary's estimation. She worked her heart out, and slogged from dawn to dusk, yet she saw very little actual proof of conversions.

She was also becoming increasingly well-known in Scotland and the rest of the world. Mary was a bit of a legend. The British Consul even sent new officers to have basic training from Mary Slessor at Ekenge. You could not dispute the fact that Mary knew how to handle people. It wasn't just native chiefs who trembled at her temper... British Officers were beaten down to size too.

Mary would chuckle at all their supplies and tools and bits and pieces. The water filters they used were simply scorned as a stupid afterthought. She was, however, very pleased if they brought supplies of tea with them!

Plague

It was only natural, being so far away from 'civilisation', that Mary would get confused now and then. Schedules were out the window, and the clock was either the sun in the sky or the hunger in your belly. Only the other week Mary had got her days all wrong. She had been so sure it was Sunday until Mr Ovens arrived from Duke Town and promptly told her that it was in fact Monday.

'Och well,' she told him, 'You will just have to have two Sundays, as I was whitewashing the house yesterday.'

Mary had recovered from more fevers than she could remember, and sometimes she just had to go back to Creek Town for a short rest. It still annoyed her that recruits were so few and far between. Her work was blossoming, more and more of the local chiefs were sending their sons and daughters to her for education, and she was the only one available to do the job. The whole mission station was being manned by the sum total of one woman. What upset Mary even more was the small number of conversions.

However, things were changing in the tribes. Mary's influence on them, as far as trade and commerce was concerned, meant that they were now moving towards the main trade route of the Cross River. Mary was glad to have the mission agree to build her a new house at Akpap where most of the tribe were now relocating.

Mary would still flit between Ekenge, Ifako and Akpap, and she had outposts in all of these areas. But Akpap would eventually become her key post and Ekenge would disappear from her circuit.

But, as always, the mission didn't move fast enough for Mary, and she decided to move her family to Akpap before the house was ready. Mary and her children moved into a cockroach infested hut. It had its fair share of rats too. But Mary was more than used to dealing with these creatures and, during the night, the family would quite often hear her grabbing her old canvas shoe and walloping it down, hard on the floor. 'Take that ye brute!' would echo around the little hut.

However, one day something attacked Mary's tribe that not even she could fight off. Mary had a good knowledge of medicine and disease. She knew most of them and the cures required, but when smallpox hit the Cross River tribes Mary began to fight a losing battle. She had to get lymph supplies from Duke Town. Then she started her vaccination programme. Hundreds came for Ma's medicine. Janie was Mary's only helper and, between them, they vaccinated for hours on end, day in, day out, until the lymph supply ran short and they had to send for more. But the news came back that there was no more to be had. Mary racked her brain; her head was beginning to hurt and her muscles ached.

'Janie, there's only one thing to do. Call back the other patients, the ones who have had the lymph injections.' Janie looked puzzled, as she picked up a water bottle from the floor, getting ready to head out to the villages.

'We may be able to rescue some of the lymph from the pus that is being secreted out of the injection wounds. If we can gather some of that together we can continue the vaccination programme for a while at least.' Janie ran quickly and headed off to the next village and the one after that.

In the days that followed, people began to realise that even Mary's medicine was not going to save them from this disease. The pile of dead corpses in the yard of Mary's house grew steadily. Those who were still well enough deserted their villages, and soon the area was like a ghost town. Only the dead and the dying were left.

Mary struggled on until the very last patient had died. Then she went to see her friend, Edem, whom she had nursed through his bout of fever. However, at the door to Edem's house, there was silence. There were no wives or slaves to be seen, no children, no animals even. The house was deserted except for the still and motionless corpse of the chief who had once been Mary's friend and protector.

Mary began to dig a grave for Edem. There was no ceremony, but Mary did her best to bury him with some dignity. She took his sword, gun and chief's staff and laid them beside his body in the shallow grave she had shovelled out underneath his hut.

Then Mary left. She would never see the village of Ekenge again. Mary struggled through the jungle, fearful of leopards, stumbling in the dark. A few days later she was found by some visiting missionaries in her bed at Akpap, filthy and exhausted, too tired to move.

***

Early in 1898, Mary finally sat back to view the new frame house that had just arrived with Mr Ovens. She was looking forward to their new home. Mary, however, soon fell ill with a fever. As she sat on the edge of her bed Janie came over to hold her hand.

'Ma, you must see it yourself? You can't walk.' You can't carry on like this. We have to do something?'

'Duke Town it is then, Janie?'

'Yes, I'm afraid so.'

And with that Mary was packed up into a canoe and taken to Duke Town where she got on a steamer for Liverpool.

'Who will look after Akpap?' asked the anxious little missionary.

'Mr Ovens has agreed to do that,' Janie soothed Mary's anxiety and settled her into her cabin.

'The other children are all right, Janie?'

'Yes, Ma. The mission has made sure they are all in good hands and Mary, Alice and Maggie are coming with us. We're all sorted.'

Mary smiled again, still unsure about leaving but knowing that there was no other choice. Janie laughed, 'You've no need to worry, Ma. Why we've even got posh clothes for the journey. The missionary barrel arrived last week and we're all kitted out smartly.'

'I don't care about smart, Janie, as long as we're warm. The weather's going to be pretty chilly once we get to Scotland.'

When they arrived at Waverley Station in Edinburgh, the chill cut through them like a knife. 'That wind. I remember that wind,' grimaced Mary, as she struggled off the train with three-year-old Alice and sixteen-month-old Maggie.

People stopped to stare at the oddly dressed woman standing on the platform, lost looking and clutching on to two little black children. A porter dashed across to them and said, with some importance, 'Miss Slessor, let me help you.'

Whispers were heard from the curious spectators, 'Mary Slessor? That's Mary Slessor.'

The whispers fluttered around the station as Mary and her brood were escorted to their waiting transport. Mary was glad to get away from the staring eyes. She hadn't realised how much of a celebrity she was in her native land.

She was still tired, still fragile but Mary couldn't wait to get home, home to Calabar.

Hippos and Cannibals

'If you don't send me back, I'll swim back!' Mary declared. She had had her fill of meetings, fundraisers and recruitment drives.

She wrote to the church newspaper about her disappointment concerning the mission. Mary believed that others should take her place, and allow her to go to the notorious cannibal tribe, the Aro.

'If missions are a failure, it is our failure and not God's,' she reminded them. So in December 1898, just after her fiftieth birthday, she returned to Calabar and the Okoyong tribe, still thinking about what her next step would be.

Soon Mary was back dispensing medicine, teaching school and sorting out squabbles. One day a tribe, who had heard about her reputation for fairness, came to ask if Ma Akamba would help them sort out a tribal dispute with the Okoyong.

'Of course!' exclaimed Mary.

The hearing was to be at the other tribe's village. So a canoe was sent for. As they scudded down the river a movement was seen in the water beneath.

Mary stared beneath the boat into the murky depths of the river. Then, crashing out of the water, came a huge, gaping mouth.

'Hippo!' was the terrified cry of the boatmen. A hippo was one of the worst animals to meet on the river. Its gaping mouth held huge white teeth, each one bigger than a gravestone. One bite could cut right through a canoe and kill all the occupants. A boatman thrust his oar into the hippo and it turned away, only to come back at them from a new direction. This time the hippo came straight at Mary.

Scared out of her wits, she picked up a cooking-pot and threw it at the hippo shouting, 'Go away you!' To the amazement of the whole crew it did.

The stories about Mary spread like wildfire and within months of the event children were re-enacting the hippo story up and down the Cross River.

As Mary continued her work with the Okoyong she continually thought about the Aro tribes. Chiefs from the Itu tribes came to ask for help. Mary saw the Itu tribe as one step closer to the Aro and agreed to set up a mission station and school in their area. But, as the mission had put a ban on further expansion, Mary had her hands tied. She could help in small ways but not in the way that the Itu tribes wanted. They were desperate for God and his Book. Mary sighed and said that she would try, but they would have to wait.

One day Mary had to help a member of her own tribe, her own little family. Janie, when barely sixteen years old, had married a young man at Mary's school. However, later that year, 1899, Janie gave birth to a little boy who died very shortly afterwards. Mary's heart bled for her when she found her one day on the doorstep. Her husband had left her. He had heard about Janie being a twin and believed that she was cursed. He would have nothing more to do with her.

That evening Mary sat out on the veranda. She needed time by herself to think. It was a never ending battle to get twins accepted in this country. She was now in her fifties and had been working over thirty years in the Calabar.

'It seems sometimes that I haven't made any headway. How do I get them to understand?'

But Mary knew that God had a plan for today, tomorrow and the future. 'I've said it before, Lord, I have to wait on you and I have to keep going. '

***

One day Mary was making her way along a trail towards the river. She wasn't going as fast as she used to. Mary's eyesight was failing and rheumatism slowed her down. As she turned the corner of the trail she peered into the distance. A fat, balding, British officer was coming in the other direction, followed by some

Efik tribesmen carrying large bundles. Mary secretly laughed at the panting official struggling up the path. 'Miss Slessor,' he gasped, 'Just the person I have come to see. I want to fill you in on the latest Aro tribe news. Things are hotting up there.'

Mary stopped to listen. It appeared that the British had uncovered the Aro tribe's great secret.

'Some of our officials picked up survivors who escaped from the Aro tribe. Apparently the Aro have made other tribes agree to worship the Aro god Chuku. Some tribes pay huge sums of money to this god but, what we didn't realise, is that over the years this god is said to have eaten hundreds of people.'

Mary urged the official to carry on. Taking a swig out of his water bottle he continued. 'Well, apparently these people weren't eaten by any god or by the Aro.'

Mary gasped, 'What? That's what I thought was happening. They are a cannibal tribe and people have always talked about the disappearances and human sacrifices that go on over there.'

'Yes, but apparently it's even more serious. The Aro are selling these people as slaves!'

Mary sighed, 'Just when I was getting the Aro to speak to me. I had some chiefs here the other week asking advice.'

The official looked surprised, 'Really? I didn't realise you were that close to them.'

'Well, yes. I know quite a few chiefs by now and they visit me at Akpap sometimes. I have been trying to get into their tribe to set up a mission for months. I suppose this will all stop now. Are you sending in the troops?'

'We will be. Troops are being gathered at Duke Town as we speak. It will be a month yet but the plan is to send in 150 white officers and several thousand troops.'

Mary's face paled. 'It's going to be a blood bath.'

The official nodded, 'I'm not sure how much of this I should be telling you.'

'Oh, don't worry,' Mary flicked a fly away from her face. 'The Aro will probably know about the soldiers by now anyway. They won't be coming out to see me since this has all blown up. But I know this tribe better than any of your officials in Duke Town. The Aro are a proud tribe, a proud people. But you have to win their trust.'

'Now, Miss Slessor, you're not going to talk anyone out of fighting this tribe. They've had their chance and it hasn't worked.'

Mary nodded, 'I know, I know... just get in touch with me if you think my way might work.' Then she carried on down the trail, frustrated and anxious about what was going to happen. The official continued to struggle – huffing and puffing as he went.

Months later the news came through that officers and troops were about to attack the Aro. All missionaries were to retreat to Duke Town.

'Why?' Mary demanded.

'Because it is not safe for you or the other missionaries. The Aro might take you as a hostage.'

'Rubbish!'

'Miss Slessor, there is no discussion about this. You are being ordered back to Duke Town. You and your family must leave immediately.'

Mary had no option. Again she was being packed off to Duke Town against her will, and this time she didn't even have as much as a temperature. She was thoroughly cheesed off!

Mary was not allowed back to Akpap for quite some time. She had to stay in Duke Town and her temper got shorter and shorter.

'I'm fed up with this place. Ever since someone worked out what was causing this malaria thing Duke Town has got awful snobbish.'

Scientists had discovered that malaria was transmitted by mosquito bites and precautions could now be taken against the disease. This meant that officials were taking their wives to live with them at

Duke Town and, as a result, some places were now no go areas for the Africans. This sickened Mary and the other missionaries. She deliberately went out of her way to upset some of the more snobbish Brits by being seen to be very friendly with African chiefs and slaves.

Eventually the battle commenced, and the whole area of the Calabar was on tenterhooks. Tribes and chiefs were anxious about what this meant for them. Would this battle have repercussions on their own relationships with the British? But then none of the Calabar tribes were particularly sorry about what was happening to the Aro. The Aro tribe sent out distress messages, asking the other tribes to come and protect them, but none came. The tribes of Calabar were fed up with the Aro and their god and the way that they had been used.

Some missionaries were sitting in the mission house along with Mary when news came through about the surrender. A British official retold the tale, 'It was a massive show of force. The Aro have been put in their place, and I don't think they will be bothering us again. No – our boys have done us proud.'

Mary sneered at the imperious gentleman. Already she was planning the quickest way to get back to Akpap.

'What is amazing though,' continued the official, 'is how little of that area we actually know. Everywhere we send in troops we find towns and villages we had no knowledge of.'

Mary grimaced, 'And how long has our mission been here?' Nobody answered that question; the answer was too embarrassing. Mary had put her finger on the problem. With just one question she had shown them the opportunities they had missed. The mission had started in Calabar in 1846, two years before Mary was born. The Calabar mission had been working for over fifty years, and yet had been totally ignorant of a vast majority of the people of its area.

Mary sighed and left the room. Heaving her old bones up the mission house stairs, she went into her room and started to fling things into bags. Soon Mary Slessor and her little tribe of children were closing the mission house doors behind them. They made their way towards the Cross River and a boat that would take them to Akpap.

'Did she ask permission?' enquired the flustered official the next day. 'All missionaries are supposed to ask permission before they return.'

'This is Mary Slessor we are talking about,' was the incredulous reply.

***

Mary was glad to be back. The Aro people had contacted her again. Mary's advice was being sought after. As no civilians were allowed into the Aro tribe's area, the Aro were sending delegates to Mary's house to speak with her. She successfully managed to calm the Aro's nerves, and they eventually agreed to accept the terms of the peace settlement. On top of this the Aro asked Mary to come and live with them.

Mary was going to have her work cut out for her. The Itu tribe were clamouring again for her attention. 'You promised us a school,' they demanded. But the work was just too much for one person. Then some amazing news came.

'Janie, Janie, look at this. The mission say that they will send us an assistant. That means, when she arrives I can spend more time with the Itu and Aro tribes. She can take on more of the duties with the Okoyong.'

It was almost too good to be true. A woman missionary, willing to leave the comforts and civilization of Duke Town to assist Miss Slessor in her work. The Mission Board couldn't believe it themselves.

However, the committee structure, as always, slowed things down. Months later there was no sign of the assistant. Mary stamped her feet and took off to spend some time with the Itu tribe anyway, leaving Okoyong under Janie's care.

Janie questioned Mary about the whole situation before she left. 'Ma, are you sure it's all right setting up the school at Itu without the mission's permission?'

'Do you realise how many years that will take? Janie, lass, we've no time. We've got work to do!'

And with that Mary was off up the river in another canoe, to see another tribe and to set up another mission station – one that her church knew absolutely nothing about. It was the first and it wouldn't be the last.

However, as she struggled to get the school started, one thought kept popping up at regular intervals. 'The Aro have still not been reached.'

But Mary struggled on with the work that she did have. This meant a lot of sailing up and down the Cross River between Akpap and the Itu tribe.

One day she rushed down the trail to catch her canoe to Itu. However, this time she missed it, which was very annoying as she would have to wait another week before visiting the Itu tribe again.

At the same time the next week, Mary was there early, waiting for the boat to come by and pick her up. 'I'd better not miss it this time,' she scolded herself. 'What's this?' Mary looked up, puzzled, at the sound of a steam boat coming up the river. It wasn't her boat; it was much bigger. As she looked she noticed a British official on board, waving at her.

'I keep bumping into these chaps,' Mary sighed. 'Oh well, I'd better speak to him, I suppose.' Mary waved as the boat drew into the side of the river. When the gentleman disembarked, he introduced himself as the British official in charge of the Aro negotiations. Mary smiled. Perhaps this was why she had missed her boat? God had been planning something all along.

When the official asked Mary if she would accompany him to the Aro tribe to help negotiate, she jumped at the chance. They were soon sailing to the very centre of the Aro tribal area, Arochuku.

As they drew near, the official gave Mary instructions. 'Be careful when you disembark. We don't want to make them nervous. We'll wait until we're introduced and take things slowly. What do you say?'

But as the boat drew near the bank, Mary jumped on shore in a flash. Immediately she was in the thick of the Aro tribespeople who were smiling and chatting to her.

'You know these people?' gasped the official.

'Yes, they've been in my house. They say they've been waiting to see me for ages and they want me to start up a school. I've said yes.'

So another 'secret' mission station was set up and all it required was Mary's enthusiasm and energy. Her tour of Calabar was expanding week by week.

Returning to the Okoyong tribe one day, Mary began to write a letter to the mission asking for an ordained minister to come out to conduct a baptism and communion service.

'I am overjoyed to finally see people who wish to commit their lives to Christ. It is such a relief to see converts.'

However, on the day, the only people to accept baptism and communion were members of Mary's family. Superstition meant that many who had asked for baptism were too scared to go through with it. Mary didn't let it get her down though. She was sure that eventually her people would come to know her God. She would just have to wait. And then finally the new assistant, Miss Wright, arrived! Now that had been well worth the wait.

***

'Ma,' asked Janie one morning, 'What's in that letter you've just got?'

Mary sighed and showed it to her.

'It says here that I am due for leave soon'

'I didn't realise it had come by so fast. What are we going to do?' Janie asked.

'Do? Do? I'm doing nothing but staying here. Who's going to take over the journeys up to the Itu and the Aro if I'm gone? Miss Wright is managing fine here and you are a great help, but if we were to go on leave, Janie, all this work would stop. I'm going to write a letter to the Board. I've a few confessions to make, I'm afraid, but now's as good a time as any.'

Mary took up her pen and began to write. She decided to come clean about all the missions and schools she had set up without the church's knowledge. She told the Board about all the expansion she had done against their wishes. Then she asked for supplies. 'If possible please send out another female missionary by the end of the year. I would much rather use up my time of leave to initiate further expansion into the Aro tribe. But if the Board has other plans I would be willing to wait to hear what they are.'

Mary gritted her teeth and sent the letter. It seemed as if she spent most of her life dragging her disgruntled and unyielding church behind her into Africa.

The agreement was finally made. Mary would continue with the expansion into the Aro tribe during her time of leave. She would do it at no extra cost to the mission.

'And how are you going to do that?' asked Janie.

'I have £100 per year as a salary. I hardly use any of it. I am sure I can save more than I have been. I live a frugal life. I can manage.' And manage she did. If it was travelling miles into the unknown, facing hostile tribes or even mixing cement, she would do it.

The travelling she was used to. Dealing with hostile tribes was a skill she had learnt and, as for cement, she just mixed it, prayed and left the setting up to God.

The Beginning

The expansion was mind-boggling even to Mary, as every tribe she met was asking for God and his Book.

Then Mary held her first service at Arochuku. She sat underneath a shady tree, the sun falling gradually from its height in the sky, and she sighed. She could see the people coming out of their huts, women, naked except for beads and chalk decorations over their bodies, children, dirty and unkempt as usual but happily chasing chickens.

Mary stood up and looked at them as they came towards her and she smiled. Lifting up her voice Mary sang, and the people listened as she slowly taught them the tune and the words. She always treasured these times when she told her people about her Lord Jesus Christ. She would look in their eyes and tell them that he had come to save the Aro tribe on the west coast of Africa. 'He loves you. God loves you,' was the message she always left with them.

And that was how Mary went on with her life – meetings, teaching, treating illnesses – but with no schedule or timetable and just a compass to make sure she could find her way home at night.

But then came the day that Mary had been dreading. She went to the edge of the Cross River and turned to look at the weeping faces of the people that she had worked for for the best part of her missionary life. Mary was now leaving the Okoyong tribe to move permanently to Itu. The Okoyong were being well provided for, and Mary knew that the Itu and Aro tribes now needed the best part of her energy. She had to focus on them.

Swarms of Okoyong came to see her off. They came with presents of yams, goats, chickens and eggs. The presents were so many that it was impossible for Mary to take them with her so they had to be left behind.

As the boat was launched out from the Ikonetu beach, a great wail was heard from the shore as the people said goodbye to their 'Ma'. Mary's eyes filled with tears. And as she lost sight of her friends, she sat down in the bottom of the boat and sobbed her heart out. For a long time she just sat there crying and wouldn't speak to anybody.

***

'The Okoyong are always in my heart,' thought Mary, 'but I have to reach out to these people too.'

Again Mary set up schools, services and clinics. She also set up a women's settlement to help women fend for themselves when they were abandoned by their husbands.

'African women can run their own lives,' Mary would say indignantly, 'if only they were given the chance. They do most of the farm work. They sell at markets too. If they were given land of their own they would be self-supporting and not so dependent on the men for their food and livelihood.'

'Is there a need, though?' she would be asked.

'Of course there's a need,' she would reply indignantly. 'I've several unwanted women propped up in my house at this moment. They've nowhere else to go!' Mary would exclaim, frustrated at people's lack of vision.

With all the extra work at Mary's women's settlement, and the visiting and travelling she had to do, a kind-hearted friend decided that she needed a bicycle to help her travel. Mary loved this, and coped with it very well before her rheumatism slowed her down. When this eventually happened she got one of the orphan boys to help push her through the bush.

However, the cycling didn't last for very much longer. Mary's health took a turn for the worse.

'I can't believe it,' Janie sobbed. 'She looks so ill and she can't move. She's completely paralysed.'

Miss Wright and other missionaries agreed that Mary had to go back to Scotland once again. This time she would go alone. Janie would stay behind to look after things. Mary returned to Scotland for what was supposed to be a twelve month leave of absence from Calabar. However, this only turned out to be five months as Mary couldn't bear to be away from her home for longer. She just had to get back to her people and her Janie.

***

When Mary returned to Itu, something momentous happened that she had been waiting to see ever since she had began work with the Calabar people. Mary was carried back through the bush by some of the tribesmen and she was singing her heart out. For the first time since she had come to Africa she had seen twins actually returned to their family with their mothers. 'It's wonderful,' she sighed, as she gazed at the stars. She remembered all these frightening journeys into the bush to save children only to find they had died in the night. She sighed when she thought about all the babies she had nursed but had had to bury in the soft earth outside her home. But now there was a success story to tell, something good to remember.

Mary hoped that there would be more, and there was. That year several women and their twins were accepted back to their families. The tide had turned, as far as the twins' problem was concerned.

But Mary was getting old. As well as having to wear false teeth her eyesight was failing. Her body couldn't cope and she was having to learn to delegate tasks. Suffering from a bad dose of dysentery Mary was eventually sent back to Duke Town. When she arrived she was reluctantly banished to her bed for complete rest.

'I am doing nothing but eating, growing fat and shedding my buttons all over the place,' Mary grumbled.

However, eventually Mary was ready and she returned to one of the mission stations under her command, the village of Use.

'Perhaps this time I will keep a little better,' she hoped. However, this was not the case, as Mary's good health only lasted for six months.

'I can't give up, though. Look at what needs to be done. The Christians in Ikpe are being persecuted, there's the murders and sickness, the orphans, and teaching and, vaccinations and services, and ...'

Mary's list would go on and on and not even her failing energy, poor health or even her doctor could persuade her to slow down.

As 1912 and 1913 came and went news filtered through of the awful casualties in Europe. But this European tragedy was far removed from Calabar and Mary looked forward to a new year and another new start. However, not long after New Year, 1915, Mary collapsed. Janie came in and found her on the floor of the hut.

'Ma, Ma!' there was no response but a muffled moan and Janie ran to get help. Gently they raised her from the floor and placed her on the bed. But even this was painful. Mary had beome so thin that lying in bed brought no comfort to her.

The mission staff took turns to look after Mary. Janie gazed for hours at the pale rugged face and then at the humble surroundings of the room. The red-brown walls were stained and crumbling slightly. The concrete floor had one or two faded rugs to hide some of the dirt. Stretching out her hand she brushed some dust off the pile of books by the bedside. The Bible lay there with its margins full of notes. The two books with Charles Morrison's signature lay underneath. Above the bed a small photograph was pinned to the wall, yellowed slightly with age and curled at the edges. Janie looked at the faces and remembered the story that she had heard so often as a child. 'That man must have been quite different as a young boy. Ma used to describe it so well – the time when he swung that lead weight past her. Now there he is in that photo with smart clothes and a cloth cap, a pretty young wife with a little child in her arms.' Janie thought about the change in that young man and the changes she had seen in other young men and women in her village. Change was a strange thing. How could one little woman bring about these changes? From the depths of her memory Janie heard Mary's voice, 'God plus one is a majority,' and she realised that it wasn't the little woman in the bed who had made the changes. It was the God she trusted and believed in. It was the power of Jesus Christ who had made a grubby little street urchin into a missionary and it was the power of Jesus Christ who had made the cannibals into lovers of God.

Janie felt that perhaps she had lived all her life with a human tornado, sweeping her along, filling her sails... and the quiet and stillness would be awful and strange. It wasn't quiet and still outside. Janie could hear the gathering crowds squeezing on to the veranda. She caught sight of some trying to peek in the windows. One of the missionaries went outside to calm things down a bit.

A tortured voice called out from the bedside, Janie rushed over to hold Mary's hand, 'Ma, Ma, it's me. It's Janie.'

'O Abassi, sana mi yok. O God release me.'

... and he did.

Janie bowed her head, tears flooding down her face. A sob caught in her throat, and she leaned over to close Mary's eyes. A rough, brown hand carressed the worn, weathered, cheek of the little missionary.

Janie then stood up straight and went to the door. Looking into the anxious, enquiring faces of the people gathered there she said simply, 'Ma is gone'

***

Then, as the flags flew at half-mast in Duke Town, on the banks of the Cross River torches shone in the night. The small wooden coffin was held high above the heads of Efik, Okoyong, Itu, Enyong, Aro and Ibibio. Her people, the people she had travelled thousands of miles to serve, were taking the little frail body of their servant on its last journey... in complete silence... no wailing or screaming of grief, no tearing of clothes or beating of breasts... just a silent mourning of deep respect.

It was their tribute to the woman who had come to tell them about the greatest servant of all, Jesus Christ, the Son of God, the Son of the God who loved them. They would never have heard about him if she hadn't come.

The following day, they buried Mary Slessor, Ma Akamba, in the dry and dusty earth beside the graves of William and Louisa Anderson. In the past the tribes had used this place to discard the bodies of their slaves. Now they buried the bodies of their missionaries there. Calabar had changed. God had worked in the hearts of these people. And part of his plan had been to use the life and skills of a little Dundee street urchin. Mary Slessor, the servant of the slave, had now gone home for good – it wasn't Scotland, it wasn't Calabar. Home is where the heart is and her heart was with him, with Jesus Christ.

Thinking Further Topics

1. The End

Which words in this short chapter tell you that Ma comes from another country? Why do you think she has come to Africa? Look at an atlas or a globe and find the continent of Africa on it. People who become missionaries have obeyed God's call to, 'Go into all the world to preach the good news,' (Mark 16:15). What is the good news? What is the good news that Jesus brings? What is it about Jesus that makes him special? God wants people to know that a life of sin is a life of slavery but a life of trusting in Jesus Christ means true freedom.

2. Fight, Fight, Fight!

What tells you that Ma in chapter one and Mary Slessor are the same person? Mary is sad about Robert's death. Do you know someone who has died? How did it make you feel? People should feel angry about death sometimes. But death is not God's fault. Death is a consequence of sin. Read the first three chapters of Genesis to find out how this happened. However, remember that everyone who dies believing in Jesus Christ will have eternal life. (John 3:16.)

3. Gossips and Bad News

What material was Dundee famous for? What was it used for? Many people went to Dundee to find jobs. If you know someone who is unemployed you should respect them for who they are. God has given everyone abilities. We should be thankful for them. Think about your abilities. Read Ecclesiastes 9:10. What does this verse tell you about yourself and about God?

4. Wishart Street

On page 20 which paragraph describes Mary as being a bit of a ruffian? Mary also longs for adventure and excitement. She wants to be a missionary, but doesn't want God to be in charge. Do you listen to authority or do you rebel against it? Do you think you know best? God should have control of our lives and we should obey him. Why? Read Romans 8:8 and discuss.

5. Africa, Canoes and Calabar

Why do missionaries do what they do? This chapter also tells us that Calabar and Dundee were difficult places to live in in the 1800s. How do you know that Calabar was a difficult place to live in? God was preparing Mary for life in Africa. Mary learnt how to survive poverty and bad living conditions. Think about your life. God may be taking you through problems to prepare you for other problems later on in life. God knows what is going on and what the future holds so trust him. Read Proverbs 3:5-6.

6. Mary's First Day

What new machinery speeded up production in the Dundee mills? How does Mary feel when she starts school and realises that God has listened to her prayers? Do you pray? The most important prayer you can pray is to ask God to forgive you. 'O Lord listen, O Lord forgive.' (Daniel 9:19)

7. On The Street

Why was Mary ashamed of being seen at the pawnbrokers? Was she right to feel ashamed? Mary and her mother are relieved to get a little money and they thank God for it. Think about your life and what you have to thank God for. Give thanks in all circumstances. (1 Thessalonians 5:18.)

8. A New Baby and a New Life

Is Mary still getting up to mischief? How can you tell? The old woman tells Mary about God and frightens her at the same time. Mary says later that she would never do something like this. However, look up Luke 23; Acts 16. Who else was brought to know Christ in a frightening way. Remember that Jesus also spoke gently and children loved him. (Mark 10: 14-16).

9. A Tea Party and a Bully

What are the main differences between Mary's home and the minister's? Mary meets a bully on her way to church. How would learning about Jesus help a bully and someone who is being bullied? Look up Luke 19: 1-10; Matthew 26:6-13; Mark 10: 13-16. Who are the bullies and who is being bullied? How does Jesus help?

10. One Tiny Missionary

When did Mary sail for Africa? What kind of lizard does she see? When she boards the ship she realises that the cargo is alcohol. This upsets her. Why? However, Mary knows that God is all-powerful. How would knowing this help you in a difficult situation? Read Psalm 147:5.

11. Ready for Anything

How did the Duke Town missionaries communicate with Creek Town on a clear day? Mary is concerned that the Africans think Jesus Christ belongs to white people only. Why is it wrong to think this? Which country was Jesus born in? Was Jesus white? Read Romans 3:23; Malachi 2:10; Daniel 7:13&14. What do these verses tell us about people?

12. Treks and Tree Climbing

Where is it that the village discussions take place? Mary was different from the other missionaries. How was she different? Some people felt it was wrong of her to climb trees. Were they right? Remember that God's word is the only rule to direct us. (Psalm 119:105; Psalm 32:8). God has made us all different. We all have different abilities and problems. The best way to live is to obey God and to enjoy him for ever.

13. Alarm Bells and Supper

What is the name of the tribe that Mary plans to see in the interior? Mary starts to learn the Efik language. This was part of God's plan. It was also God's plan for Mary to befriend the slave girls. Mary could sympathise with them. How could she do that? Jesus sympathises with us as well. Read Hebrews 4:14-16 and find out how he does this.

14. Malaria and a Journey

What medicine was given to Mary to treat her malaria? Mary found it difficult when her plans didn't succeed. Do your plans ever fail? How would trusting in God help you feel better? Sometimes our plans don't succeed because God knows they are wrong or it is not the right time. 'My times are in your hands.' (Psalm 31:15)

15. A Midnight Adventure

Who does Mary try to rescue from the forest? The tribes people are very superstitious. Mary finds this difficult particularly when the people kill and harm young babies and children. Read Deuteronomy 18:10-13 to find out what God thinks about superstition. If you are worried about your future what should you do? Read 1 Peter 5:7 to find out. 'For I know the plans I have for you,' declares the Lord, 'plans to prosper you and not to harm you, plans to give you a hope and a future.' (Jeremiah 29:11)

16. Double Trouble

What nickname does Mary have? Do you remember some of the other nicknames she had when she was younger? When Mary's mother and sisters die she is very sad. When Mary's brother died Mary was not only sad but angry too. Do you remember what it was about her mother that puzzled her then? In this chapter she says that heaven is closer now than Britain. How can she say this? Who is in heaven now that makes this true for her? (1 Peter 3:22; Psalm 139:8.)

17. Boiling Oil

What did Mary do to make sure the men swallowed their medicine? Mary becomes known for standing up against injustice. Do you remember another time when Mary stood up to bullies? Mary experienced God's help in dangerous situations. Can you think of times when you have had to stand up against bullies? Were you afraid? What does God say to people who are afraid? (Deuteronomy 20:1, Psalm 27:1; Mark 5:36.)

18. Mary Meets Her Match

Which part of Mary's services did the Okoyong like the best? Who stood up to Mary and refused to let her out of the hut? Mary had regrets in her life too. She regretted that Edem and Eme never turned away from idols to worship the one true God. Do you have regrets from your life? Do you ever wish you had done something differently? You will never regret trusting Jesus Christ. God is always listening. 'The eyes of the Lord are on the righteous and his ears are attentive to their cry.' (Psalm 34:15.)

19. Romance at last?

What is the name of the young man that Mary meets in Duke Town? When her fiancé can't come to work with the Okoyong the engagement is broken off. Mary's adopted children go on to get married and have children of their own. Recently Mary's great-great grandchildren have even come back to Scotland to study. They thank God for Mary and her witness in Nigeria. If she hadn't come these young men and women wouldn't be alive today. Do you think about getting married some day? Whether yo do or not it is important to realise that there is one that you should love more than anyone else in the world. 'Love the Lord your God with all your heart and with all your soul and with all your mind.' (Matthew 22:37.)

20. Back on Track

Mary is now an experienced missionary and she is getting older. How old is Mary when she writes her report? Mary is now respected by the Africans. They trust her and know that she is fair. They ask her for advice – because she has gained their trust. Is it hard to gain trust and respect? What do you have to do to gain someone's trust? Why is it important to be respected when telling others about Christ? 1 Timothy 3 gives a list of the ways a Christian should behave.

21. Plague

What is the main trade route out of Calabar? Mary has to tackle the plague and many people die. It was an upsetting time for her. Read Genesis chapter 3. Why do you think that people fall ill and die? Romans 6:23 says that the wages of sin is death but the gift of God is eternal life. Christians aren't exempt from sickness and death. But we can turn to God for comfort. Read Jeremiah 31:13.

22. Hippos and Cannibals

What did Mary throw at the hippo? Mary realises that she has to wait for God's time and that actions will convince the people when words won't. What actions can you do to show God's love? What action did God do to show how much he loved us? (see John 3:16) Read John 15:13. Do you think this is true? Can you name anyone who did this?

23. The Beginning

What presents did the Okoyong bring Mary when she left? Mary's funeral showed how God has changed the people of Calabar. What effect will your life have on people? Do you think that people see you as different because you love Jesus? If you don't love him remember Jesus is the only way to heaven. (John 14:6) Why do you think that this chapter isn't the end of Mary's story but only the beginning? (John 11:25&26; 1 Timothy 4:8; Job 19: 25-27.)

Facts on Nigeria

Nigeria is a federal republic in West Africa. The country has been called the *Giant of Africa*. It became a democracy in 1999. Major cities include the capital Abuja, the former capital Lagos, Ibadan, Osogbo, Calabar, and Benin City.

Nigeria is on the Gulf of Guinea and its major cities are located in the south. The central area of the country has hills and plateaus. The north has dry plains bordering the Sahara. Nigeria's neighbours are Benin, Niger, Chad and Cameroon. The Niger Delta is one of the largest river systems in the world. The country's main export is oil.

Nigeria has a population of 135 million people, making it the country with the highest population in Africa. The life expectancy is approximately 47 years. About 68 per cent of the population are literate.

The official language is English. Other languages include: Hausa, Yoruba, Igbo, Fulani. French is also widely spoken.

The religions of the country are: Muslim 50%, Christian 40%, and other beliefs 10%.

Nigeria has over 250 ethnic groups, all with 4,000 dialects. The three largest are the Hausa-Fulani who are in the north, the Igbo who are in the southeast, and the Yoruba who are in the southwest. The Hausa tend to be Muslim and the Ibo, Christian.

Bible translation is still a major challenge. The Bible Society of Nigeria, the Nigeria Bible Translation Trust and other denominations and agencies have made a great deal of progress, but there are still approximately 379 languages without the Scriptures..

Mary Slessor: Life Summary

Mary was born in Aberdeen and moved to Dundee aged eleven. Her father was a shoemaker who was also an alcoholic. He eventually became a mill labourer. Mary's mother was a godly woman and attended church regularly. Mary also became a Christian. And as a young woman she joined a local mission that was involved in teaching the poor. She became well known for her courageous spirit. Once she even dared a gang of boys that she would not flinch as they swung a metal weight closer and closer to her face. She successfully stayed still and the boys had to attend her Sunday School as forfeit.

In 1876, she applied to the Foreign Mission Board of the United Presbyterian Church of Scotland. She was briefly trained before being sent to Calabar. It was a time of turmoil in Nigeria. Murders and human sacrifice were all common. Women had no rights at all and were considered as low as animals. Superstition was rife. This particularly effected the safety of baby twins - who were often accused of being demon possessed and left to die. Mary took these abandoned children into her own family home to save them from being sacrificed.

Mary suffered from flu and malaria in Africa as vaccinations for smallpox and other diseases were not yet available.

Mary shocked many missionaries by living with the locals. She learned to speak Efik fluently and became familiar with the local customs and culture. Her close understanding of the Nigerians led the local Governor to offer her a position on the Itu court.

Mary Slessor received the Order of St John of Jerusalem in 1913. Recurring illness made her very weak and in 1915 she died of a fever. She was buried in Nigeria after a full state funeral.

Mary Slessor Time Line

1848 **Mary Slessor born.**
Wyatt Earp, later U.S. Marshall, born in
Monmouth, Illinois. U.S.

1850 Telegraph cable laid from Dover to Calais.
Baking powder invented.

1854 Abraham Lincoln makes first political speech.

1856 End of Crimean War.

1858 **Mary moves to Dundee.**

1861 American Civil War begins.

1863 Football Association founded.

1871 Stanley finds Livingstone in Africa.

1876 **Mary is sent to Calabar.**
Alexander Graham Bell invents telephone.

1880 Mosquito found to be the carrier of Malaria.

1888 **Mary goes to the Okoyong.**
Van Gogh paints 'Sunflowers'.

1892 **Mary made Vice Consul in Okoyong.**

1899 Aspirin invented.

1903 Henry Ford sets up his motor company.

1905 **Mary named Vice President of native
court.**
Einstein publishes theory of relativity.

1911 Amundsen reaches the South Pole.

1913 **Mary receives Order of St. John of
Jerusalem.**

1914 First World War begins.

1915 **Mary Slessor dies.**

1918 First World War ends.

TRAILBLAZER SERIES

Gladys Aylward, No Mountain too High
ISBN 978-1-85792-594-4

Corrie ten Boom, The Watchmaker's Daughter
ISBN 978-1-85792-116-8

Bill Bright, Dare to be Different
ISBN 978-1-85792-945-4

John Bunyan, The Journey of a Pilgrim
ISBN 978-1-84550-458-8

Amy Carmichael, Rescuer by Night
ISBN 978-1-85792-946-1

John Calvin, After Darkness Light
ISBN 978-1-84550-084-9

Jonathan Edwards, America's Genius
ISBN 978-1-84550-329-1

Michael Faraday, Spiritual Dynamo
ISBN 978-1-84550-156-3

Billy Graham, Just Get Up Out Of Your Seat
ISBN 978-1-84550-095-5

Adoniram Judson, Danger on the Streets of Gold
ISBN 978-1-85792-660-6

Isobel Kuhn, Lights in Lisuland
ISBN 978-1-85792-610-1

C.S. Lewis, The Storyteller
ISBN 978-1-85792-487-9

George Müller, The Children's Champion
ISBN 978-1-85792-549-4

John Newton, A Slave Set Free
ISBN 978-1-85792-834-1

John Paton, A South Sea Island Rescue
ISBN 978-1-85792-852-5

Helen Roseveare, On His Majesty's Service
ISBN 978-1-84550-259-1

Patricia St. John, The Story Behind the Stories
ISBN 978-1-84550-328-4

Joni Eareckson Tada, Swimming against the Tide
ISBN 978-1-85792-833-4

Hudson Taylor, An Adventure Begins
ISBN 978-1-85792-423-7

William Wilberforce, The Freedom Fighter
ISBN 978-1-85792-371-1

Richard Wurmbrand, A Voice in the Dark
ISBN 978-1- 85792-298-1

THE JUNGLE DOCTOR SERIES

1.   Jungle Doctor and the Whirlwind
        978-1-84550-296-6

2.   Jungle Doctor on the Hop
        978-1-84550-297-3

3.   Jungle Doctor Spots a Leopard
        978-1-84550-301-7

4.   Jungle Doctor's Crooked Dealings
        978-1-84550-299-7

5.   Jungle Doctor's Enemies
        978-1-84550-300-0

6.   Jungle Doctor in Slippery Places
        978-1-84550-298-0

7.   Jungle Doctor's Africa
        978-1-84550-388-8

8.   Jungle Doctor on Safari
        978-1-84550-391-8

9.   Jungle Doctor Meets a Lion
        978-1-84550-392-5

10.   Eyes on Jungle Doctor
        978-1-84550-393-2

11.   Jungle Doctor Stings a Scorpion
        978-1-84550-390-1

12.   Jungle Doctor Pulls a Leg
        978-1-84550-389-5

13.   Jungle Doctor Looks for Trouble
        978-1-84550-499-1

14.   Jungle Doctor Operates
        978-1-84550-500-4

15.   Jungle Doctor to the Rescue
        978-1-84550-516-5

16.   Jungle Doctor Attacks Witchcraft
        978-1-84550-517-2

17.   Jungle Doctor Goes West
        978-1-84550-595-0

18.   Jungle Doctor Sees Red
        978-1-84550-501-1

19.   Jungle Doctor's Case Book
        978-1-84550-502-8

The Adventures Series
An ideal series to collect

Have you ever wanted to visit the rainforest? Have you ever longed to sail down the Amazon river? Would you just love to go on Safari in Africa? Well these books can help you imagine that you are actually there.

Pioneer missionaries retell their amazing adventures and encounters with animals and nature. In the Amazon you will discover tree frogs, piranha fish and electric eels. In the Rainforest you will be amazed at the armadillo and the toucan. In the blistering heat of the African Savannah you will come across lions and elephants and hyenas. And you will discover how God is at work in these amazing environments.

African Adventures by Dick Anderson
ISBN 978-1-85792-807-5

African Adventures by Dick Anderson
ISBN 978-1-85792-807-5

Amazon Adventures by Horace Banner
ISBN 978-1-85792-440-4

Cambodian Adventures by Donna Vann
ISBN 978-1-84550-474-8

Great Barrier Reef Adventures by Jim Cromarty
ISBN 978-1-84550-068-9

Himalayan Adventures by Penny Reeve
ISBN 978-1-84550-080-1

Kiwi Adventures by Bartha Hill
ISBN 978-1-84550-282-9

New York City Adventures by Donna Vann
ISBN 978-1-84550-546-2

Outback Adventures by Jim Cromarty
ISBN 978-1-85792-974-4

Pacific Adventures by Jim Cromarty
ISBN 978-1-84550-475-5

Rainforest Adventures by Horace Banner
ISBN 978-1-85792-627-9

Rocky Mountain Adventures by Betty Swinford
ISBN 978-1-85792-962-1

Scottish Highland Adventures by
Catherine Mackenzie
ISBN 978-1-84550-281-2

Wild West Adventures by Donna Vann
ISBN 978-1-84550-065-8

CHRISTIAN FOCUS PUBLICATIONS

Christian Focus | Christian Heritage | CF4K | Mentor

Christian Focus Publications publishes books for adults and children under its four main imprints: Christian Focus, Christian Heritage, CF4K and Mentor. Our books reflect that God's word is reliable and Jesus is the way to know him, and live for ever with him.

Our children's publication list includes a Sunday school curriculum that covers pre-school to early teens; puzzle and activity books. We also publish personal and family devotional titles, biographies and inspirational stories that children will love.

If you are looking for quality Bible teaching for children then we have an excellent range of Bible story and age specific theological books.

From pre-school to teenage fiction, we have it covered!

Find us at our web page:
www.christianfocus.com

CF4·K
Because you're never
too young to know Jesus